# Building Academic Literacy

# Building Academic Literacy

*Engaging All Learners in Every Classroom*

Janet Angelis
Karen Polsinelli
Eija Rougle
Johanna Shogan

ROWMAN & LITTLEFIELD
Lanham • Boulder • New York • London

Published by Rowman & Littlefield
A wholly owned subsidiary of The Rowman & Littlefield Publishing Group, Inc.
4501 Forbes Boulevard, Suite 200, Lanham, Maryland 20706
www.rowman.com

Unit A, Whitacre Mews, 26-34 Stannary Street, London SE11 4AB

Copyright © 2016 by Janet Angelis, Karen Polsinelli, Eija Rougle, Johanna Shogan

*All rights reserved.* No part of this book may be reproduced in any form or by any electronic or mechanical means, including information storage and retrieval systems, without written permission from the publisher, except by a reviewer who may quote passages in a review.

British Library Cataloguing in Publication Information Available

**Library of Congress Cataloging-in-Publication Data**

Names: Angelis, Janet I., author.
Title: Building academic literacy : engaging all learners in every classroom / Janet Angelis, Karen Polsinelli, Eija Rougle, Johanna Shogan.
Description: Lanham, Maryland : Rowman & Littlefield, 2016. | Includes bibliographical references.
Identifiers: LCCN 2015040509 (print) | LCCN 2015048626 (ebook) | ISBN 9781475823264 (hardback : alk. paper) | ISBN 9781475823271 (pbk. : alk. paper) | ISBN 9781475823288 (electronic)
Subjects: LCSH: Language arts—Correlation with content subjects. | Literacy. | Critical thinking.
Classification: LCC LB1576 .A55 2016 (print) | LCC LB1576 (ebook) | DDC 372.6—dc23
LC record available at http://lccn.loc.gov/2015040509

∞ ™ The paper used in this publication meets the minimum requirements of American National Standard for Information Sciences Permanence of Paper for Printed Library Materials, ANSI/NISO Z39.48-1992.

Printed in the United States of America

To all the teachers with whom we have worked and without whom this book would not be possible.

# Contents

| | |
|---|---:|
| Foreword | ix |
| Preface | xiii |
| Acknowledgments | xix |
| **1** Purposeful Pedagogy: Developing Each Mind | 1 |
| **2** Purposeful Engagement: Activities to Engage and Support All Learners | 27 |
| **3** Purposeful Talk: A Framework for Facilitating Academic Discussions | 57 |
| **4** Purposeful Experiences: Assignments to Sustain Thinking and Learning | 89 |
| **5** Purposeful Planning: Designing a Coherent and Connected Curriculum | 123 |
| **6** Purposeful Leadership: Supporting Effective Instructional Practices | 141 |
| Conclusion | 157 |
| Appendix A: Sample Lessons | 159 |
| Appendix B: Further Reading | 169 |

Literary Works Cited 173
Bibliography 175

# Foreword

The Partnership for Literacy is a very exciting professional development and literacy instruction project across the grades and across school subjects. It was born from the research, and continues to be a component of, the Center on English Learning & Achievement (CELA,www.albany.edu/cela).

Taking the best of what was already 15 years of CELA research on literacy learning, as well as related research on literacy and professional development within the field, into instructional development studies, Arthur Applebee, Martin Nystrand, and I developed a program of teaching and learning based on the theories we had already developed.

We did this in collaboration with a team of superb teacher educators and teachers who developed the instructional activities to produce such a successful program that after the research project had ended, the schools didn't want us to leave, and new schools invited us to work with them. Thus, since 2002, the Partnership has continued to operate and further refine its offerings based on school and district needs and the changing demands of educational policy.

Why call it the Partnership? We call it a partnership because we see it as a true partnership, where each of the participants is valued as having a unique and critical role, voice, and commitment to the success of their work together. The partners are the teachers, the students, the administrators, and the coaches. They work as a team. The coaches bring the research to the teachers and administrators in ways that make the activities cohere, for added impact.

The teachers and administrators help the coaches understand their students and their instructional context in ways that help the coaches select materials and focus the activities to intensify that impact. The students are invited into the activities as participants, expected not only to engage in the learning activities but also to reflect on them and provide feedback about their learning, questions, and needs, thus rounding out the partnership and adding impact.

How does the Partnership work? We see learning as an ongoing lifetime activity, even learning about teaching. We also see teaching as an ongoing lifetime activity that is supported by a web of models, supports, and interactions around a core of inviting and substantive content. These supports aid learning for people of all ages. Therefore, we engage teachers in the kinds of activities they plan to use with their students (sometimes using professional readings and other high- or low-technology experiences; sometimes, research findings; and sometimes, classroom material and activities).

Throughout the engagement, we help them reflect on their own experiences, cognitive moves, and learning and on what an activity or approach might mean for their own students' learning experiences. We not only give them new activities but also new ways to organize those activities for purposes of higher-content literacy learning and to "read" their students' needs—both for added impact.

The authors of this book have done a superb job of presenting all this and more to their readers in a lively format suffused with examples of classrooms-in-action, activities for students, and activities for teachers, thereby inviting readers to experience the partnership as active and engaged readers. It's a wonderful experience that I invite you to enjoy and to take away and use.

Here's to engaged and enjoyable learning for all!

Judith A. Langer<br>
Vincent O'Leary Distinguished Research Professor<br>
Director, Center on English Learning and Achievement<br>
School of Education, University at Albany

# Preface

> *Any knowledge that doesn't lead to new questions quickly dies out: It fails to maintain the temperature required for sustaining life.*[1]

We often begin a workshop for educators with the above quote; we ask them to reflect on what it means to them and then discuss their various thoughts and perspectives, focusing in particular on its implications for classroom instruction. Over the years, we have found this to be a provocative exercise.

This quotation always opens up a fruitful examination of and dialogue about the nature of teaching and learning. It prompts educators at all levels to consider the kinds of questions that sustain student engagement so that students gain the kind of knowledge and skills they need in order to become successful in future schooling and in life—in other words, to become college and career ready.

## WHY WE WROTE THIS BOOK

We have been privileged to witness and help teachers create classroom environments that open up multiple pathways for students to become active learners and thinkers. These classrooms are what internationally known literacy researcher and scholar Judith Langer describes as "minds on"[2]—that is, teachers and students together create dynamic communities of thought and learning that continually expand students' knowledge and skills. Students read, research, discuss, and write with purpose and power.

The classroom is not confined by its walls nor defined by static chunks of content. Rather, teachers use content as the "stepping off place" for students to dig deeper and connect with the world outside, including with parents, the community, scholars in a particular field, and each other. They are alive with knowledge seeking and learning in a dynamic, organic process guided by the teacher but very much owned by the students. The temperature is indeed right for sustaining life.

Like those who propose building professional learning communities among teachers, we have long advocated that teachers develop *classroom* learning communities that invite students to play an active role in their learning process. Teachers who have done so enjoy classrooms in which they and their students engage in wondering, hypothesizing, researching, and thinking about the content of the curriculum.

Their fortunate students have gained the kind of knowledge and skills called for in the Common Core State Standards. Rather than lecturing and dispensing knowledge, these teachers facilitate a process in which students both individually and collectively become actively engaged in seeking and generating knowledge, learning to think and write like authors, historians, mathematicians, scientists, artists, and so on, depending on the area of study. "They construct knowledge; they don't swallow it."[3] And they learn in cooperation with each other rather than at the expense of one another.

Like some of us, you may have begun your teaching career with such a vision of the learning process but may not have had support to enact it in your particular setting. Or you may have changed your vision of teaching and learning over time and may now be seeking more engagement and learning from your students. Or you may be expected to teach to the Common Core State Standards, which call for more higher-order thinking, application of knowledge, and comprehension of more complex and informational texts.

Perhaps you and/or your colleagues feel stuck in "test prep" mode and hope to find a more meaningful way to prepare students to be successful on their high-stakes tests while still enjoying learning and gaining the broad base of knowledge they need for the years ahead. Or perhaps you are a principal or other instructional leader responsible for supporting teachers wanting and/or needing to make these changes. In any of these cases, you may not be quite sure about which instructional tools will accomplish what you are looking for and may not have access to a coach to guide you or the teachers you support.

With this book, we are hoping to be that "coach-in-a-pocket." We make suggestions, tell you why these suggestions should work, ask questions to help you reflect on teaching and learning and troubleshoot when something falls short (it will), and provide the pacing to help you keep one foot in the familiar while taking small but deliberate steps toward a new vision of an exciting classroom in which to teach and learn.

Although we suggest certain activities, we are less concerned with the particular tools and activities than with supporting both teachers and students to get to the big ideas and big-picture thinking that ensure learning. Teachers who have taken that chance with us not only produce students who gain literacy in their content-area subjects, but they find renewed joy and purpose in their own teaching. By sharing what we have been observing in thinking classrooms, our goals are no less than that for our readers.

## WHO WE ARE

We are all teachers ourselves. Together we have spent nearly a century in classrooms from pre-K to postsecondary and have taught English, mathematics, social studies, science, foreign language, and technology. Currently we serve as leaders and coaches in the Partnership for Literacy in the University at Albany's School of Education. In addition to Dr. Langer, we worked with Dr. Arthur Applebee; with Langer, Applebee, and others, including classroom teachers, we developed the Partnership for Literacy.

For more than a decade, we have worked in dozens of schools, coaching teachers and instructional coaches individually, as well as in teams and departments, to adopt the ways of teaching and thinking about teaching that we share in this book. These methods have been validated through decades of research by Langer, Applebee, and others in schools and classrooms across the country. We describe this research briefly below and suggest sources for more-detailed information in the annotated bibliography.

Janet is the associate director of the Partnership, and Karen, Eija, and Johanna are coaches. Johanna and Karen learned and further developed these practices when they took part in one of the foundational studies of the Partnership as classroom teachers with Eija as their coach. Then, as now, they were partners in the project. We call our project the Partnership for Literacy because we work in partnership with teachers; we start with what teachers and principals want to try to change or their own goals for student learning and then work with them to plan ways to accomplish those goals, asking questions, listening, and suggesting.

Although in a book we cannot hear your responses to the questions we raise for you to consider, we would like to be partners in your quest. We begin by assuming that you are interested in finding ways to guide your students to higher levels of thinking and achievement and to take more interest in and greater ownership of their own literacy and learning. And we assume that you would like to find ways to help them use literacy more effectively so they can learn more and become more skilled in the process.

## OUR RESEARCH BASE

Throughout the text we offer brief explanations of why we suggest a particular tool or activity based on what the research tells us about how people learn. One of the things research has shown is that instruction is most effective when teachers have both a conceptual understanding of why a tool works as well as the pedagogical knowledge to make it work.[4] Therefore, we think it is important to explain why—to provide a brief but basic explanation of the theoretical foundation that supports everything we recommend.

Fundamentally, we understand learning to be influenced by context—it is a social activity. Therefore, thinking, writing, and talking together are essential elements of effective classrooms. And since learning means connecting new knowledge to old, coherence matters. For those who want to know more about related theory and research, we invite you to explore Appendix B, an annotated list of resources that we encourage you to turn to whenever you feel you want to learn more about the underlying research or find additional information on a topic.

## NOTES

1. Wislawa Szymborska, "The Poet and the World," lecture, Nobel Prize in Literature Ceremony, Stockholm, Sweden, December 7, 1996.

2. Judith A. Langer, *Getting to Excellent: How to Create Better Schools* (New York: Teachers College Press, 2004), and *Envisioning Knowledge: Building Literacy in the Academic Disciplines* (New York: Teachers College Press, 2011).

3. Susan Engel, "Playing to Learn," *New York Times*, February 2, 2010, http://www.nytimes.com/2010/02/02/opinion/02engel.html.

4. Pamela L. Grossman, Peter Smagorinsky, and Sheila Valencia, "Appropriating Tools for Teaching English: A Theoretical Framework for Research on Learning to Teach," *American Journal of Education* 108, no. 1 (1999): 1–29.

# Acknowledgments

The work we represent in this book rests on the shoulders of countless others—the researchers whose investigations we have learned from; our colleagues, including teachers we have worked alongside; administrators who offered support along the way; and friends and family who endured our crazy schedules and long hours.

We especially want to thank those who led the Center on English Learning & Achievement (CELA), where the ideas presented in this book were tested and found to work: Judith Langer and Arthur Applebee and colleagues at the University at Albany and Martin Nystrand and colleagues at the University of Wisconsin–Madison. Not only did they lead and oversee the research of CELA, but their ongoing research, writing, and leadership taught us much about the whys and wherefores of effective instruction.

Working alongside us in developing and testing these ideas were Mary Adler, Eileen Kaiser, Samantha Coughlin, Ester Helmar Salasoo, and Barbara Ring. Together we partnered with teachers to try new tools and activities, then measured their impact on student learning. We thank them as well as Kathy Nickson, who for many years joined us in bringing these ideas to additional schools, grades, and teachers.

Besides the fact that we have promised anonymity to our teacher partners, it would be impossible to name the hundreds who have been teaching us and learning from and with us. Together we all strive to engage students in minds-on classrooms that continually develop and hone their abilities to understand and represent all that they learn in all of their subjects.

Thank you also to those whose early reviews of our manuscript made it stronger. We benefited from early reviews by Arthur, Judith, and Kathy and from more recent reviews by Lynn Lisy-Macan, Kathy Cotugno-Surin, Susan Tangorre, Nancy Andress, Michael Angelis, and Kevin Kelly. We would also like to express our appreciation to our editors at Rowman & Littlefield: Tom Koerner, Carlie Wall, and Jessica McCleary. Thank you, everyone.

*Chapter One*

# Purposeful Pedagogy

*Developing Each Mind*

> *Remember then that there is only one important time, and that time is now. The most important one is always the one you are with. And the most important thing is to do good for the one who is standing at your side. For these, my dear boy, are the answers to what is most important in the world. This is why we are here.* [1]

In the quotation above, artist and illustrator Jon Muth is responding to Tolstoy, who said that there are only three important questions in life: Who is the most important person? When is the most important time? And what is the most important thing to be doing? Muth must also be a teacher, for isn't this what teachers do every day—determine how to help each child in front of them succeed?

So what does this book have to do with Muth's cross-century dialogue with Tolstoy? It offers a process for establishing a classroom in which each student each day is at the center, a classroom where teachers craft scaffolds to bring each student to higher-order thinking in the content area(s) that they teach. This task is great, the expectations greater still, and the consequences of failing are daunting.

This book is designed to be a "coach-in-a-pocket" to help any teacher do good for every student before them; it will help you problem solve, try out, and create lessons and units on overarching topics that will make your classroom buzz with the shared expectation that every child has something to contribute—and will. In other words, it is a guide to developing every mind.

Here are the meanings of some key words:

*Purposeful pedagogy.* Pedagogy that is purposeful deliberately develops each mind. Teachers who practice it have an overall expectation for learning, and they understand each student. In considering the content they are responsible for teaching, they order and pace it and provide opportunities for students to try on thinking as a biologist or mathematician or historian or writer might. They design student learning opportunities so that students gain knowledge and ways of thinking not only for today but for tomorrow and next week and next month and next year.

With the 21st Century Learning Skills and Common Core State Standards (CCSS) in mind, these teachers seek to prepare students for productive and fulfilling futures—for a world no one today can yet clearly see. They help every student not only become ready for college or a career but also to learn how to learn, in other words, to be prepared for life beyond school—no matter what educational or career paths they might choose. If you are an educator, the responsibility of preparing students in this way is yours.

*Literacy.* In this book, literacy refers to academic literacy, which means using language and thought effectively not only in English language arts (ELA) but also in multiple disciplines. This includes learning the specific ways of thinking and knowing in any discipline—that is, developing expertise as a historian or scientist would.

The CCSS are demanding such content or academic literacy by calling for more rigorous engagement with academic content for all students, as well as developing students' ability to process and share their understanding orally and in writing. Literacy, then, means not just reading, but writing, speaking, listening, and thinking. Because literacy is essential to students' future success and because the CCSS focus on literacy, literacy is a major focus of this book.

*Higher-order thinking.* Higher-order thinking entails deciphering texts, comparing them, synthesizing and evaluating them, looking for evidence, examining the authority of the writer to express ideas and interpretations, and thinking across texts and disciplines to have a greater perspective in appreciating the worth and value of ideas. Teaching this kind of thinking requires careful scaffolding and choice of materials and texts (both print and nonprint) that accommodate different learning styles and encourage overt means of making thinking visible, including extended writing.

One of the most powerful tools to develop higher-order thinking skills is to use student talk as the center of classroom instruction, to develop and channel that talk into meaningful academic discussions by using a model for discussion that guides students to ever-higher levels of thinking. Teachers who use this model to facilitate student conversation teach students to wrestle with complex texts and concepts, as called for in the CCSS. Discussion works![2]

Harnessing the social interactions so important to adolescents and building a classroom learning community that highlights student thinking results in all students with minds on the work at hand, engaging discussions, and thoughtful writing about big-picture ideas. This can happen in every content area, across every grade level, and *in every kind of school.*

This book will show you how to do this. It asks you to tap your creativity and experience as a teacher as it guides you in planning and enacting instruction that pushes students to the higher levels of thinking, learning, and academic literacy now required.

## HOW TO USE THIS BOOK

The general flow of each chapter is an explanation of the topic and why it matters. Throughout each chapter you will find examples drawn from actual classrooms,[3] which vary by grade and subject. You will get the most out of these classroom descriptions if you read them as if entering into a conversation with them, looking for inspiration for how something might look and work in *your* school or *your* classroom with *your* students and *your* subject(s). Most examples come from the core subjects (especially social studies, science, math, and ELA) but a few are from other subjects like home and career or health.

Then comes a "try it" part that suggests a specific tool or activity to use. It is always best to first try something yourself so that you know what it feels like (this will be even more effective if you try an activity with a partner or partners); put yourself in the learner position before you bring an activity to your student-learners. Whatever you do, please do not pull out any activity or tool just before a lesson and attempt to use it! Rather, read about it while you are planning, consider the suggestions, and figure out when and how you can weave it into an upcoming lesson.

The proposed activities are not just engaging—not a set of gimmicks or tricks, if you will—but are well-designed and tested approaches that engage learners in disciplined thinking about a topic. They employ what is known from cognitive science about how the mind works. Rather than naming specific material to use, the examples suggest the *kind* of text to try something with—guidance for you to select materials suitable for your content area, age group, and curriculum topic.

After you have tried an activity, return to the book and use the prompts provided to reflect on how it went and what you will do next. If all went as planned and you are pleased with what your students accomplished, you are ready to either use the approach again with different material or try the next suggestion.

If you are less than satisfied with the result or if things went awry, please read the "Troubleshooting" section to see if it has anticipated your particular situation. Then with that information as guidance, plan to try the approach again with different material—again fitting it into your ongoing instruction and again reflecting on results and deciding next steps. The intent is to help you create a richer classroom in which every student is thinking, writing, reading, listening, and talking in order to learn more about and become more literate in the content.

Each tool or activity is designed to build on or extend those that came earlier—or on ones that you already may use. However, there is no end to how often you can use any instructional strategy. As you include any new approach in your instruction, you will find yourself improving it, deepening it, helping your students get more out of it. All of the activities are enduring instructional approaches, and you may already be using some. Include those that work best for you as part of your regular repertoire.

To give but one example: If you routinely go over homework questions with the whole class, it is hard to know what most students are thinking or even if they are paying close attention. A variety of techniques can engage all students in the review while you monitor their work and gain detailed knowledge of the thinking and learning of individuals, thus accomplishing the same goal but with more of the students engaged more of the time. Additionally, you will become more knowledgeable about individual student's learning and needs.

In fact, one purpose of everything suggested is to have all students engaged and thinking all of the time—no student on the sidelines. This coach-in-a-pocket will guide you to adopt and adapt tried-and-true practices that others have used to create thoughtful and effective learning environments in whatever subject(s) you teach. In so doing, you can have all students in your classroom minds on and learning the content in ways that will endure.

## Key Elements

Each chapter covers a key element of effective curriculum and instruction. In addition to serving as an introduction, Chapter 1 addresses the need to provide a classroom environment in which every student feels safe to voice her or his thoughts; it also includes some activities designed to lay that necessary foundation. Chapters 2–5 address primarily classroom teachers, and Chapter 6 addresses primarily those charged with supporting effective instruction (e.g., principals, instructional coaches, department chairs), offering tips and guidance for those who have read the earlier material.

In addition to "Opening the Classroom to Student Voice" (part of Chapter 1), then, the key elements include

- *purposeful engagement:* capturing all minds and providing instructional scaffolds to develop higher-level thinking (Chapter 2)
- *purposeful talk:* facilitating classroom discussions that connect every student to content, deepen their thinking, and build academic literacy (Chapter 3)
- *purposeful experiences:* providing meaningful opportunities for students to learn and share their thinking about the content (Chapter 4)
- *purposeful planning:* rethinking curriculum to be coherent and coordinated (Chapter 5)
- *purposeful leadership:* supporting teachers as they try the approaches offered in Chapters 1–5 (Chapter 6)

The kind of classrooms described in the pages that follow do not develop overnight. Students will not know quite what to do or how to behave if a teacher makes a sudden switch in instructional approach. Therefore, the chapters are organized to lead you through a progression of activities. By following these activities you will build a strong(er) foundation for an inclusive classroom in which every student is expected to actively engage and is encouraged and feels safe to fully participate. As you then keep developing and refining your approach, you will achieve ever-stronger thinking and learning.

## Common Threads

Through every chapter of the book you will find four common threads. All are essential to an effective classroom, all require an active role on the teacher's part, and all are critical to preparing students for college and a career. These threads are

- the reading-writing-speaking-listening-thinking connection
- academic literacies
- higher-order thinking, including critical thinking and reflection
- equity

*The Reading-Writing-Speaking-Listening-Thinking Connection*

The introduction to the Common Core Standards includes the statement, "In short, students who meet the Standards develop the skills in reading, writing, speaking, and listening that are the foundation for any creative and purposeful expression in language."[4]

Because all aspects of literacy are connected and each can be used to support the further development of the others, all of the activities suggested in this book connect student talk to reading and/or writing while "upping the ante" on thinking. Since learning is a social activity, classroom talk is a natural tool to use to promote engagement and learning and to connect them to reading, writing, listening, and thinking; yet student talk is generally an un- or under-tapped resource.[5]

*Academic Literacies*

The CCSS are unusual among recent reform efforts in that they recognize that literacy is not a generic term. Rather, there are multiple literacies; in terms of academics, each discipline has its own ways of knowing, thinking, and doing. The CCSS call for students to be "proficient in reading complex informational text independently in a variety of content areas."[6] Therefore, another common thread is the need to explicitly teach students how to acquire and share knowledge like scientists or mathematicians or historians, and so on.

## Higher-Order Thinking, Including Critical Thinking and Reflection

Although the terms *critical thinking* and *higher-order thinking* are often used interchangeably, thinking critically is one aspect of higher-order thinking and refers to the way people analyze and interpret information. And it can be taught.[7] Thinking critically can also refer to reflecting on and analyzing one's own thinking and performance. Teaching students to think about their thinking helps them to acknowledge their strengths, address their weaknesses, and demonstrate independence. Reflection helps to create learners who will not only be successful in school but will be able to participate and contribute to the world beyond school.

## Equity

The CCSS call for improving access to rigorous academic content for all students, including those for whom English is not their first language and those with special needs. Because intelligence is not fixed but dynamic, it is imperative that you invite all students into the work of the classroom and expect that all can contribute.[8]

Inviting all students into meaningful classroom work requires providing academic and/or social scaffolds (supports). Good scaffolds ensure not only full participation but also that everyone benefits from the ideas and perspectives of all; a diversity of voices asking questions and suggesting answers builds every student's understanding and helps develop the ability to understand other views and to think critically. This does not mean one-size-fits-all instruction or treating all students exactly the same; rather, instruction should differentiate by offering multiple entry points so that all students can engage and participate. This book will show you how.

The next section opens with two scenarios that offer a vision of classrooms in which every student is able to talk about a topic that matters. These scenarios demonstrate what is meant by student "voice" and why it is advantageous to you and your students that they be able to express their thinking. The final section of the chapter provides some guidance for teaching students how to talk and think together by paying attention to five classroom essentials.

## OPENING THE CLASSROOM TO STUDENT THINKING AND VOICE

What you envision when you imagine a classroom makes a difference in how you set up and manage your own classroom. Do you see straight rows of students facing a teacher who is standing in front of the room either asking questions or conveying information, maybe using a SMART board or other technology? A few students' hands may be up, but most students are sitting quietly and you cannot gauge their level of engagement.

The minds of some students may have escaped the classroom altogether. Have you spotted the girl with her eyes cast down? Follow her gaze to the open book in her bag. It appears that her mind is no longer in the classroom. Lost to her are both the teacher's questions and classmates' answers. The promise of a story on the book's pages is apparently what excites the child and engages her mind.

Or do you see instead a classroom in which every student is working? Desks have been pushed together in clusters to support small group discussions. Students have texts and writing materials spread on the desks. They are talking and discussing points they want to make for a presentation to the class. They are checking the content to evaluate whether it supports their argument.

Students recheck texts, bring ideas to the table, argue, and abandon some ideas as they converse, writing down any new ideas or evidence and facts in their notebooks. Voices mix and mingle, ideas grow, and arguments are shaped. Ideas pulled from the content are bounced back and forth and scrutinized, with some dropped altogether and some revisited and sharpened with more evidence.

You can hear the teacher saying, "Keep thinking!" as she moves between the groups, sitting in, listening to the arguments and ideas taking shape, and encouraging more fact checking. Students, too, move around as they need to, to get books or journals or to consult a computer or the teacher and to discuss a point with fellow classmates. Through their joint work, each presentation is taking shape. All students are engaged, and no student's mind has escaped the classroom.

The first scenario is a familiar image still seen all too often. The teacher controls both the talk and the thinking; even if he or she is using new technologies that ask every student to display his or her answer, the questions lead students toward one correct answer—the one the teacher is looking for.

In the second scenario, the teacher expects that all of the students, every single one, will think and learn together. The classroom is flexible and inviting, buzzing with ideas about the topic at hand. Good thinking is noticed and encouraged. Everybody is engaged mindfully in reading, writing, and talking about the content, listening to each other's ideas about the content and what it means. Because there is to be a presentation, students know that their team's work counts—ideas from each group will be recorded and presented to the class community.

Which scenario better prepares students for their future work and world? The one in which they are expected to simply produce the correct answer or the one in which they are taught to use content to collaborate about important ideas? The choice seems obvious. Students who are college and career ready need to be prepared in classrooms that resemble the second scenario, classrooms in which reading, writing, listening, thinking, and talking are critical for performance and are at the center of instruction.

For students to be able to share their thinking with peers and teachers, they must feel emotionally safe, so it is essential to make the classroom a safe place for students to take the risks necessary for high-level learning. The activities suggested in this book support students to voice their thoughts, concerns, and questions in writing and in discussion with peers so that they become accustomed to thinking together.

Student voice and teacher voice are critical tools for learning. Voice is the expression of a writer's or speaker's thoughts, intentions, and interpretations at any moment. Voices express social worlds and identities and mediate emotions and meanings. Creative classrooms that are rich in students' voices are open and authentic and invite a multitude of perspectives.[9]

Teachers in such classrooms use *their* voices purposefully to orchestrate and scaffold students' growing understandings. All of these voices interact and mix and generate new ideas and meanings in a dialogic fashion. Voice is critical to thinking and learning.

*How much student motivation and engagement matter was recently demonstrated in an urban English as a Second Language (ESL) classroom. Jane*[10] *had decided to use storytelling as a primary vehicle for helping her English language learners learn not just English but also the elements of story, part of the state curriculum and included on the state ELA assessment. She invited Johanna to tell some stories, and Jane and her students also read stories from around the world, sometimes from the students' homelands.*

*Then Jane put students in small groups to work on a story of their own, which could be based on some they had heard or read at home or in school. As she guided that process, she came to realize that the dynamics of her classroom were shifting dramatically: Each student was finding, developing, and using his or her voice. They were all coming to feel that they belonged in the class and in the school; most significantly, the student who for two years had been unwilling to speak in any class in any language was now speaking all the time—in English. His classmates had held his feet to the fire, so to speak.*

*He was as responsible as any other group member for his part of the story—beginning, middle, or end—and they did not give him a pass if he did not know a word. They needed his contribution for their story to work; he knew it and made the effort to fulfill their expectations. Not only did these immigrant students gain more English-speaking skills and become more comfortable voicing their ideas, they learned the craft and elements of a story, which enabled every student to meet the state standards, some with distinction, on the state ELA assessment that year.*

This much-abbreviated vignette shows the powerful effect that having a voice, feeling connected, and playing an important role in the workings of the classroom can have on engaging students in the hard work of learning. Others confirm this. For example, *Reading Next*, the Carnegie Corporation's report on adolescent literacy, puts motivation close to the top of the list of key instructional elements of effective literacy programs for adolescents.[11]

Motivation—and the engagement that results—matters so much, in part because if preadolescent and adolescent students are not engaged, they will not do what you ask them to do, although the more compliant may go through the motions. Without engagement, they won't get the practice they need, and without practice, they won't further develop critical skills and gain the knowledge they need.

Furthermore, the motivation-engagement-achievement cycle can be vicious if it goes in a negative direction because disengaged students fall further and further behind. The entry point to turn a cycle from negative to positive must be engagement, and it is the job of instruction to engage the mind. The classroom setting offers an opportunity to take advantage of young adolescents' social tendencies in order to engage them in productive interactions with their peers in a community of learners.

The next and final section of this chapter offers five essentials that must be in place if you hope to have a productively engaged classroom.

## SECURE THE FOUNDATION BY TEACHING STUDENTS *HOW* TO TALK AND THINK TOGETHER

Consider your classroom. Are students comfortable raising questions that reveal a lack of understanding of a topic or assignment? Do their discussions wrestle with the content? Do they listen respectfully and respond respectfully to opposing views?

The latter can be difficult for adults, and your students may not have good models for respectful discussions with opposing views, so you will need to teach them. In particular, five essentials need to be in place in order to support students to learn how to take part in productive academic discussions that help them learn the content as well as the necessary speaking and listening skills.

### Five Essentials of Productive Classroom Discussions

#### 1. Students Need to See Each Other

If classroom desks are arranged in rows so that students are looking at the backs of each other's heads, it will be hard for them to make and maintain the eye contact that fosters interaction. If at all possible, rearrange the furniture so that they can see one another. Some teachers do this by grouping desks or creating a horseshoe; others have the space to set aside part of the room to which they can move for discussions; yet others have put tennis balls on the legs of chairs so that students can easily, quickly, and quietly move their chairs into a large circle.

Teachers who absolutely cannot move the furniture may need to ask students to stand for brief periods of discussion time so that they can face one another. It is essential to foster making eye contact and addressing peers in order to develop a learning community in which all students are participants and shareholders. Another option is to hold a fishbowl discussion, which allows a smaller group of students (those sitting in an inner circle—the fishbowl) to hold the discussion while others listen and take notes—switching roles, of course, to give all a turn in the fishbowl. (See the vignette below.)

One thing that helps students realize the importance of the circle is having teacher(s) sit in the circle with them. If you walk around, stand outside of or even in the circle, or sit at your desk away from the conversation, you become the focal point of the "discussion," and the circle loses its dynamic. When you share the circle, you send the message that everyone is expected to contribute and that what they have to say is so important that you don't want to miss a moment of it.

> Julio liked to teach from his desk, so when he first tried circle discussions with his fifth-grade science class, he sat at his desk while the students were all in the circle. He would ask a question from his desk, then find himself drawn to the discussion so that he left his desk and stood in the circle alongside the students' desks. He then returned to his desk and asked another question.

Again drawn to the student discussion, he eventually pulled up a chair and sat alongside the students in the circle. At the end of one class he acknowledged to Johanna, "I see why you want them to be in the circle. But I need to be in the circle, too!" Besides signaling to his students that he, too, was part of their learning community, merely by his presence in the circle he "upped the ante" in terms of expectations for student behavior, thinking, and participation.

## 2. Establish Ground Rules for Discussion

When working with any group, even adults (e.g., school improvement teams), good facilitators start by establishing the ground rules for their time together. They make the rules explicit, even if they think that all adults should know them. Do the same for your students.

These rules will work best—and will be more effectively monitored and followed—if you take the time to develop them with your students. To do this, start by asking students to think about and then jot down what they think the qualities of a good conversation are or what they think worked and did not work about a particular discussion. For example, "Referring to our discussion about [last week's storm] how did it help you learn or understand more about [weather patterns]? Did anything about the discussion interfere with your learning? If so, what?"

Follow this by asking students to individually generate two lists: on one, they list what was positive about a good conversation or the discussion in question; on the other, they list what can make a good conversation go wrong or what was negative about a particular discussion. Then have pairs of students compare their lists before sharing their findings with the whole group.

Draw on this discussion to ask the group to develop a ground rule that either reinforces the good aspect or addresses the negative. Students can refine this list over time as they become more skillful discussants. For an example of discussion ground rules that Johanna developed with her classes, see the accompanying discussion guidelines.

Discussion Guidelines

- One person talks at a time.
- Listen with an open mind.
- Treat each other with respect.
- Separate opinion/fact.
- Try to understand the opinions of others.
- Challenge the opinion, not the person.

*3. Teach "Conversation Vocabulary"*

Another helpful tool to provide your students is a list of the words and phrases they can use to enter a conversation. These can include such phrases as

- I agree with what you said because . . .
- I'm not sure I understand what you mean. Can you provide an example that will help make it clearer to me?
- I respectfully disagree with what you said because . . .
- I have a different idea . . .
- I'd like to add to (or piggy back on) your idea . . .

Depending on the grade(s) you teach, you may choose to simply provide these phrases—modeling them and posting them so that all can see—or develop a similar list with your students, following a process like that suggested for establishing the ground rules (above). Giving students the language for these phrases can have an enormously positive impact on the quality of their discussions.

## 4. Practice Discussion in Pairs and Small Groups

Paired activities (such as the Think-Pair-Share activity introduced in Chapter 2) help students practice talking with one other student about the substance of the work before sharing their thinking with a wider group. You can extend this by forming trios and/or having two pairs join up and do something more with the assignment that was assigned to pairs.

When moving students from working in pairs to larger groups, it is important that the task demand something more than the original one and be meaty and interesting enough to engage them. You can monitor that as you move around the room, listening to the quality of the conversations and to who is participating, as well as for good ideas and questions that you will ask them to bring to the attention of the whole class. Such small group work gives students practice in participating in academic discussions.

> Following a reading of the short story "Charles," Cathy asked pairs of students in her ELA class to come up with one question about the story that the whole class should discuss. The story implies that the naughty Charles, whose antics are reported by a young student to his parents each evening, may indeed be the student himself.
>
> Cathy followed the paired activity by merging pairs into groups of four to six students. Her instructions to the small groups were to put their best thinking forward by again writing a single question after discussing the ones written by the pairs. Each small group now had to wrestle with two or three potentially competing ideas, discuss those ideas, and synthesize or eliminate the ideas.
>
> As they worked, Cathy moved around the room, encouraging where needed, sending them back to the text for evidence, pushing them to dig deeper, and so on. Students grouped and refined the questions in their small group discussions, getting

> to the essence of the story in the process—using and developing higher-order skills such as classifying and independently holding an academic discussion. When the small groups were ready, Cathy wrote each group's question on the board to structure the whole-class discussion.

## 5. Have Students Reflect on the Process

Students will own what they help build. It is important at the beginning and then periodically to give them time to reflect on classroom procedures, for example, how discussions are affecting their learning and whether they are following their own guidelines.

Please resist the temptation to save time by assigning reflection as homework. Reflection needs a gentle introduction, which is perhaps best done by simply asking, "What did you think of [the discussion or activity] and the participation following it?" or "How did using [this instructional strategy] deepen your understanding of _____?" Giving some time for students to think about their thinking is truly not a luxury but is essential to helping them become independent learners.

Introducing reflection by using a paired discussion or brief written reflection followed by discussion works well. The time given does not have to be long—ask students to turn to a partner and talk about the one thing that is sticking in their minds because of a particular discussion. Have two or three students share their thinking with the whole class. Short, repeated exposures like this to reflective thinking can help foster critical thinking and an expectation that the classroom is minds on and students are responsible for their own learning.

Also, sharing your own thoughts on the dynamics you witnessed and that seem significant to you may help students see your expectations and understand them more fully.

Another way to reinforce the importance of thinking about their thinking is to ask students to keep a learning log. Learning logs or journals in each subject area help students internalize the ways of thinking and doing in that discipline (as called for in the CCSS) and develop the habit of writing to learn. Encouraging them to use technology for this, perhaps a blog, online journal, even an area of a social networking page, might foster a habit of reflecting on thinking and learning.

*Because Johanna's Grade 7 ELA classes generally numbered 28–30 students, she realized she had to find a way to have thoughtful conversations in which all students could participate and feel they had made a meaningful contribution. She had observed that when she held a full class discussion, each student might have had a chance to speak just once, maybe twice. And their comments tended all to be "stand alone" comments that introduced a new idea; they were not having real conversations about the ELA curriculum.*

*For example, in discussing an Indian fable called "A Lesson for Kings," a set of students' consecutive comments were:*

**Alice:**[12] *How could everyone say he's perfect?*

**Karrie:** *This is boring. This is a poor way to find out who's better.*

**Cat:** *There's no end to this. Did you leave half the story on the copy machine?*

*In addition, Johanna did not feel that she was doing enough to help students gain the skills and knowledge the state would assess them on each year: listening, reading, writing, and demonstrating knowledge about various genres and uses of language, as well as thinking and analyzing texts across genres. So she decided to try something different the next year.*

*First, early in September she facilitated a discussion with each class that led to their joint development of the discussion guidelines (shown above), as well as the conversation vocabulary to assist students as they took the floor. She collected suggestions from each class, then each class reflected on and revised the statements, sorting them out and making good rules that could apply for their class as well as her other classes.*

*She wrote both the discussion guidelines and the conversation vocabulary on large chart paper and hung them on wires that spread across the room so that each time they had a conversation they could refer to them as guideposts. She had thus established the basics, but she soon found that was not enough. There were still too few student-to-student dialogues.*

*So she decided to try a fishbowl to encourage students to not only "take the floor" more often but to talk with each other about their developing ideas. When she switched to the fishbowl format, she found that because she spoke less, all of the students were speaking more—several more times each in a class period—and that instead of each one bringing in a new thought, they were more focused on what the student before them had said.*

*They began to go deeper into a text, challenging it, supporting it, questioning it, and wondering more about what the writer may have intended by including a particular fact or statement. For example, in January they began a discussion of two texts across two genres, a poem and a chapter from a nonfiction book, both on the theme of families and children. The poem ("from 'Unveiled'") focused on gender favoritism in Middle Eastern cultures, and the chapter ("The Indian Child") came from a history of Native Americans.*

*She invited 15 students to start the discussion by bringing a chair into a small circle; in addition, she brought a chair for herself and a chair for a "guest." The effect on discussion was imme-*

diate. Here's a sample from an early fishbowl from one class in which students were discussing "The Indian Child":

**David:** *Since they were here first, why do they need to bend to our standards?*

**Maria:** *I agree with David. We shouldn't have them change their ways to please us.*

**Ally:** *I agree. In "The Indian Child," Indian children seemed happier than they do today. We have sadness and depression. If we shared with them, together we'd be stronger.*

**Erica:** *Ally is probably right, we both have depression.*

The other half of students had brought their chairs to form an outer circle and were listening to the inner circle's discussion. Johanna asked those students to jot down notes regarding three things in particular: (1) ideas they were hearing, (2) ideas that challenged their own, and (3) questions they wanted to bring to their own conversation, which would come in the next phase. If any student in the outer circle wished to add an idea to the ongoing discussion, she or he could occupy the guest chair, make that contribution, and then return to the outer circle.

The class usually completed both phases of a fishbowl in one period, but in this case Johanna had planned the discussion over two days. The second day's conversation began with the students who had been listening coming to the inner circle and offering a summary of the main ideas presented the day before and giving additional insights. For example, in responding to David's comment of the day before, Jerrod said, "I want to go back to David. The time before Europeans came, Native Americans needed to know how to survive. They didn't need math."

The students now in the outer circle were charged with listening, noting where new ideas might challenge their own, and/or identifying ideas that were not being brought up. The guest chair remained open for anyone from the outer circle to occupy temporarily. On the second day, six students came into the guest chair, all to comment on "from 'Unveiled'" and the role of mothers. One student even began, "This is a response to gender," because he felt that the discussion in the fish bowl was omitting that idea.

The reason Johanna added the guest chair to the inner circle was that she had learned that students in the outer circle were frustrated by being excluded from the initial conversation. Providing for a guest enabled students to respectfully enter the inner circle briefly (no longer than two minutes) to contribute to the flow of the conversation. This way all students were able to take part.

Before leaving the inner circle, each group of students had to write down something someone had said that had changed their thinking or jot down their own thoughts at the end of the conversation. When she was satisfied that the students had more fully explored the texts and had come to an increased understanding of their meaning, genres, points of view, and so on, Johanna then reflected on the discussion, asking herself how well the students had demonstrated the ways of thinking, knowing, and doing in reading and discussing literary works.

Finally, to conclude the lesson, she asked all of the students to reflect on the process of the fishbowl and how it had helped them better understand the texts and how to analyze poetry. Their responses to this reflection revealed a deeper understanding and questioning than she had seen in prior years, and the students embraced the challenges of closely reading difficult texts. They realized that what they had been practicing since September was becoming routine in the classroom, and they were more prepared to write.

About a week following the discussion, Johanna asked students to return to the two texts and, now that they had a little distance from the discussion, to write about what they felt was important for *them to consider in raising children today. Their responses were thoughtful and deep, their ideas supported with textual evidence from the two texts as well as others. She was impressed with the level of maturity and seriousness they displayed in their writing and felt they had turned a corner in becoming a classroom of literate learners—her overall goal for the year.*

## Reflection and Action

As Johanna did, think about discussions in your classroom and ask yourself to what extent your students

- talk *with each other*—genuinely question and converse with each other (not just with you)
- together grapple with ideas essential to the content
- respect each other's ideas and follow the conventions of polite discourse—that is, seem to know how to enter into a discussion and express areas of agreement/disagreement
- involve all students, including English language learners and special education students

If your reflection concludes that the characteristics above do not describe discussions in your class(es), take the time—it will be well worth it in the end—to teach the skills of effective discussion. It will build a stronger foundation for classroom interactions that will support collaborative thinking and learning. Use activities like those suggested above and in the chapters that follow with a variety of content.

And be sure to include time for reflection so that your students have an opportunity to evaluate the process and product of their discussions. This reflection is essential to their assuming responsibility for the productivity of the classroom and their own learning and will help to produce more independent learners.

## SUMMARY

Chapter 1 focuses on inviting all students into academic classroom discussions. Engaging students in purposeful conversation is the foundation of promoting academic literacy and higher-order thinking. In particular, this chapter offers five essential guides to help implement this complex learning process. Turn to Chapter 2 for more activities designed to actively engage students' minds and promote thinking and learning.

## NOTES

1. Jon J. Muth, *The Three Questions* (New York: Scholastic, 2002), based on Tolstoy's "Three Questions," available in collections of his fables or online at http://www.online-literature.com/tolstoy/2736.

2. Arthur N. Applebee et al., "Discussion-Based Approaches to Developing Understanding: Classroom Instruction and Student Performance in Middle and High School English," *American Education Research Journal* 40, no. 3 (Fall 2003): 685–730; Thomas Newkirk, "Teachers: Know When to Stop Talking," *Education Week*, July 28, 2015, http://www.edweek.org/ew/articles/2015/07/28/teachers-know-when-to-stop-talking.html?qs=july+28,+2015+inmeta:gsaentity_Source%2520URL%2520entities%3DEducation%2520Week%2520Articles+inmeta:genre%3DOpinion+inmeta:Authors%3DThomas%2520Newkirk.

3. Except when citing a published article authored by the teacher(s) mentioned, all teachers' names are pseudonyms.

4. Common Core State Standards Initiative, *Common Core State Standards for English Language Arts and Literacy in History/Social Studies, Science, and Technical Subjects* (Washington, DC: National Governors Association and Council of Chief State School Officers, 2010), 3.

5. Martin Nystrand, *Opening Dialogue: Understanding the Dynamics of Language and Learning in the English Classroom* (New York: Teachers College Press, 1996).

6. Ibid., 4.

7. Philip C. Abrami et al., "Strategies for Teaching Students to Think Critically: A Meta-Analysis," *Review of Educational Research* 85, no. 2 (2015): 275–314.

8. Carol Dweck, *Mindset: The New Psychology of Success*. (New York: Random House, 2006).

9. Mikhail Bakhtin, *The Dialogic Imagination: Four Essays* (Austin: University of Texas Press, 1992).

10. See note 3.

11. Gina Biancarosa and Catherine E. Snow, *Reading Next—a Vision for Action and Research in Middle and High School Literacy: A Report to the Carnegie Corporation of New York* (Washington, DC: Alliance for Excellent Education, 2004).

12. All student names are pseudonyms.

*Chapter Two*

# Purposeful Engagement

*Activities to Engage and Support All Learners*

> Rather than plant my thoughts into students, I have learned how to engage students in discussion that pulls their thoughts out for further examination and learning.[1]

The teacher quoted above is well on her way to building a classroom learning community in which she purposefully engages students in ways that enhance learning. She understands not only that she must hear what students are thinking to know if they are engaged and learning but also that they need to practice talking about their thinking if they are to meet the Common Core Standards. This is especially important for students who need to develop language skills and academic language, in particular.

Your students may be at very different levels when it comes to knowing how to conduct themselves in productive academic discussions. Some may need to find their voices by first learning to have one-on-one conversations with a peer; others may be ready to hold their own in a full class discussion. They all need practice doing both, as well as discussing in small groups.[2] Modeling a discussion for them is also important.

This chapter suggests some activities (e.g., Journal Jot, Think-Pair-Share, Written Conversation, reader's marks, Pass the Hat) to get students thinking and talking with peers in academically appropriate ways as they grapple with learning the content. Here and throughout this book, an *activity* refers to an experience or set of experiences that engage learners and purposefully lead them toward developing a particular body of knowledge, skills, and/or concepts (e.g., facilitating a classroom discussion on appropriate rules for classroom discussion). *Tools* are devices used to help an activity be successful (e.g., the guidelines for discussion).

Your purpose, of course, is always to have students learning and developing the knowledge and skills that are part of your overall plan. The activities and tools suggested will complement your usual methods of instruction and are designed to

- give all students a chance to voice their thoughts and thus connect and build/rehearse their understanding about a topic
- get students accustomed to sharing their thinking with peers in productive ways
- let you hear what your students are thinking and understanding about the content in the moment so that you can adjust instruction on the spot—effective and efficient formative assessment

The first few activities introduced build on those suggested in Chapter 1 to foster a climate in which students are comfortable voicing their thoughts about the topics they are studying. Then come additional tools and activities to improve students' preparation for class by promoting more careful and analytical reading of their texts. Here, as elsewhere in this book, *text* means any visual or auditory material or experience from which you want students to learn.

You may find that you already use some of the tools and activities described, but you may also find some new purposes for using them. They are a powerful and necessary way to get students to voice their thinking. Of constant concern is always engaging every student in learning, promoting higher-order thinking, and further developing language skills. Purposefully following this book's suggestions will do all of this.

Be mindful, though, that students are well schooled in the ways of school. Most are cautious and self-conscious about their ignorance, wanting to give the "right" answer; and they are not generally risk takers. Yet educators today are charged with producing innovative thinkers (e.g., by the drafters of the Standards and the earlier Partnership for 21st Century Skills) who, by definition, are risk takers. The activities recommended help create an environment in which students feel safe taking the risks necessary to think and learn together in a supportive community of learners, regardless of their individual language skills.

Researchers now know that not only is higher-order thinking critical for all students, including those for whom school is challenging, but also that educators need not wait until students have mastered the "basics" before working to develop those higher-order skills.[3] When used purposefully, the activities in this chapter will help you ensure that all of your students have opportunities to develop those higher-order skills by engaging with and learning the content while practicing using academic language.

## SHARING THINKING ONE-ON-ONE

The activities in the first part of the chapter build on each other to engage students intellectually and push them to think more critically. These—and all other—approaches should be woven together to build content learning and literacy. None are meant to be used as stand-alone activities; rather, they are most effective when they are used often and in tandem to advance understanding and drive learning deeper.

The more you use these activities, the more effective you will become, resulting in your students becoming more engaged with the content and more skilled. As you use them, you will find more ways to adapt them to different topics and tasks within your subject area(s).

## Journal Jot/Quick Write and Think-Pair-Share

You likely have little difficulty in getting students in Grades 4–8 to talk with each other, but without structure or scaffolding provided by you, that talk can quickly become meaningless academically. By pairing two activities, Journal Jot/Quick Write and Think-Pair-Share, you can use writing to prepare each individual student for a conversation with a peer. This is especially helpful for students who are learning English. It is critical to keep students focused by giving them specific time limits and instructions to discuss what they have written. These instructions are necessary scaffolds in teaching them how to conduct academic discussions in pairs or small groups.

### *Journal Jot/Quick Write*

The next time you plan to discuss a short reading, math puzzle, chart explanation, video clip, or similar material, try this: *before* asking them *your* questions, ask students to take two minutes (or another, specific but brief time period) to individually do a Journal Jot[4]—a short piece of writing that responds to one question or prompt (you might even call this a tweet, but be sure that the prompt is one that will advance the curricular content).

This is *not* writing that you will grade, but it will be public, and you may want to allow students to represent their thinking in pictures or symbols as well as words. The question should require students to voice their *thinking* about the text, not restate the factual content. To avoid a simple recall of facts, you might consider giving them any one of the following or other, similar writing prompts: "One thing I am wondering about after reading this text/viewing this video/going to the museum is . . . ."[5] Or ask a question like, "What in this text/photo/video stood out for you as especially important or interesting? Why?"

While they are writing, observe them at work, nudging and offering help when needed. As you do so, what do you notice about

- their behavior as they write (whether are they engaged, appear to be really thinking, or are distracted)
- the amount of the page they are filling
- whether they are writing the entire time or stopping early

*Think-Pair-Share*

Partnership for Literacy coaches are now seeing more Pair-Share used in classrooms but seldom see the thinking time to start it off. A Journal Jot or Quick Write provides that thinking time. When the thinking/writing time is up, ask students to share their writing with a partner and discuss *what they wrote in common* and *what was different*. (Be sure to display this and other prompts so students can refer to them if needed.) If you think you need to model this for them, see "Troubleshooting" below. Give them a specific time limit for this discussion.

When sharing time is up or discussion has waned, ask every pair to report

- what each had been thinking
- what they noticed about their partner's response and any questions that response raised

As it is here, Think-Pair-Share is best used as a step toward something else. It is meant to be a brief activity to help students engage, focus, and gather thoughts in preparation for a larger discussion, writing assignment, reading, or viewing.

If this activity has met your purpose, you may simply capture their responses on a white board or chart paper as you listen to the kind of thinking their comments reveal. Be careful to not evaluate their individual responses, although summarizing what they have said can bring this activity to a satisfactory close. Or you may want to move on to a small group or whole class discussion of the ideas they have raised (see below).

## Reflection and Action

You can use the responses students share to analyze

- what they understood about the material
- if they missed any key ideas
- the level of thinking revealed by their questions
- whether the activity met your purpose

Then you can decide on how much more scaffolding they need in order to talk productively one on one; think especially about students who need more practice with academic discussions. How will you use student responses to shape your next lesson? See "Troubleshooting" below if they had trouble with this process.

Think-Pair-Share always helps make later conversations more effective by giving all students time to collect their thoughts before speaking. Use the Journal Jot and Think-Pair-Share again with other material, refining it as needed. After the next session, again reflect on what students' comments revealed about their learning and thinking and how comfortable they are in sharing their thoughts aloud. These activities are not gimmicks. They can (and should) be used often to engage students in thinking about what they are learning; doing so transfers to students some of the responsibility for the learning that takes place in your classroom.

## Troubleshooting Journal Jot and Think-Pair-Share

**What if some students didn't write anything for the journal jot?** As students wrote, did you constantly scan the room to see if everyone was writing? If you can, this is best done while moving around the room so that you can easily and naturally stop by the desk of a student who is not writing and find out why. You may need to clarify the prompt, ask a question or two or begin a sentence to help get the student started, reassure the student to not worry about spelling and punctuation, or even suggest that she or he draw an image if that will make it easier to express his or her thinking.

If any of your students are especially reluctant writers, you will soon want to extend Think-Pair-Share into a written conversation (discussed below). There is nothing like having an audience of a peer to encourage students to write their thoughts.

**What if some of your pairings didn't seem to work?** There are many ways to assign working pairs, and you may need to experiment. It is important early in the year to set the expectation that students will routinely work together and with everyone in the room. You might couple a more facile learner or reader with one who struggles or perhaps one student who is more verbal with a student who is more quiet or who is learning English, or perhaps two quiet students might work together well. Learning which arrangements will work best with any class can require some trial and error. And sometimes random pairings will not only be productive but provide insight into who works well together.

Another consideration is that students may not be clear about what is expected of them. Do not assume that they can do all that you ask of them immediately. One way to make the task clearer for students is to model what you want them to do. For Think-Pair-Share, find a partner (it can be a student) with whom to demonstrate a good Think-Pair-Share. Have each student reflect on what they noticed, especially what was good about the sharing.

After reflecting individually, have students share their findings with partners and then draw out what they noticed onto a larger chart so that you might reference it throughout the year. Sometimes students forget how an activity should work, but with the chart always visible in the room, you and the students can refer to it and understand the shared expectations for a Think-Pair-Share. If need be, have the class create guidelines for a Think-Pair-Share. Write them large on chart paper that you can post for all to see and refer to throughout the year.

### *What if the pairs go off task and off topic?*

- The first place to look is at the text to see if it is appropriate. Questions to ask yourself include: Does this material energize me? Is it engaging? Is it ambiguous or complex? Does it leave room for more thought and questions? Does it relate in some way to what the students already know so that they have a way to connect with it?
- If you haven't already done so, (re)consider your pairings (see above); you may want to switch to or from stronger/weaker student pairings to improve productivity.
- Another area to examine is timing: Did you give students a specific time frame? Was it too long? You can always call time whenever it seems that most pairs have completed their assignment, and you'll get better at estimating exactly how long students need to have a meaningful exchange.
- Also look at the question or questions that you asked them to consider. Were they focused enough?

In general, then, four items—appropriateness of the material, pairing of students, specific time expectations with what will happen in that time frame, and one to two focused questions—can help teachers tighten up loose ends in a Think-Pair-Share session.

***What if students seemed afraid to express their doubts and questions?*** Your students may have become so accustomed to needing to know the "right" answer that they do not feel safe voicing what they do not know or are wondering about. You can help by modeling that. When appropriate, voice out loud one of your wonderings that has been prompted by an assignment (e.g., "I'm not sure what the author thinks is the most important information in that paragraph; what do you think?" "When I first read this book/story, I thought the protagonist was going to do X; boy, was I wrong!")

When students express what they are wondering, they are truly using their own voices—and giving you insight into their level of understanding of the curricular content.

## Extending Think-Pair-Share to Written Conversations about Content

When your students have become comfortable voicing their thoughts and changing their minds in Think-Pair-Share writing—rewriting their new thinking or extending their original thought—it is time to introduce Written Conversation. In a Written Conversation, all students write to the same prompt simultaneously, then in pairs or small groups (of four to five) they swap papers or electronic text files; comment on their partners' thoughts by adding, agreeing, disagreeing, and saying why; and repeat the process.

You and your students may be quite adept at e-mail exchanges and text messages, and you may certainly use those technologies for this writing/thinking tool. However, before assuming that students can simply use their familiar texting processes, remember that the intent of a Written Conversation is to be a thoughtful exploration of one's own and others' thinking about content in a particular discipline. Then consider how you can scaffold students to adapt their use of texting for primarily social purposes to something substantive. How much leeway you allow in terms of the typical texting shorthand is up "2 u" and/or your department or school policies.

You will need to set a time limit, which you can increase over time in order to build stamina; and you need to indicate a minimum number of times (two to three) they must swap. Even reluctant writers cannot resist this activity, as they get to write to peers. Because it is so appealing, students write more and in the process develop more fluency, as well as more complex understanding of the topic. Savvy teachers allow some oral conversation when it complements the writing and enables students to clarify what a partner has written; this is especially helpful for students who need practice better articulating their thoughts in writing.

These Written Conversations also lend themselves to interactive media. For example, you might assign pairs or small groups of students to exchange their thoughts via e-mail and bring the result to class. If you have set up a wiki or blog for your class, you might assign the sharing as homework; you can monitor the online participation to the extent needed and begin class with a quick summary or a request for questions.

The best prompts for Written Conversations require students to express their own thinking—not simply retelling something but reformulating it in the terms and forms appropriate to the subject being discussed. If you are a math teacher, you might try this with a prompt that asks students to explain how they solved a problem. If you can pair or group students who used different approaches, the questions and comments of the partner(s) in a written conversation can force each writer to greater clarity—good practice in developing rigor in writing and preparation for your state's assessment, too.

In social studies, photos and political cartoons provide food for thought and writing and are especially good for an introduction to the process of a Written Conversation. One example comes from a social studies teacher Johanna worked with. Dan showed his students a photo of a young Civil War soldier and asked them to write about who they thought he was, then swap papers with a partner and each comment on the other's thoughts.⁶ Another good writing prompt for a Written Conversation is to ask students to explain in writing what they think a political cartoon from the era they are studying means.

In music or art, students can write about their interpretations of a work, perhaps drawing images to depict what a piece of music means to them. And of course, history—and some scientific theories—lend themselves to arguments that can be explored in this way. You might ask students to indicate their positions and then pair students with differing views. In these cases, one requirement should be using evidence to support each person's position.

In science, Written Conversation lends itself to hypothesizing—predicting the outcome of an experiment, for example. When material seems relatively straightforward and factual, a question that asks students about implications can get them thinking. If they understand photosynthesis, for example, you might ask what effect the increasing level of smog in China is likely to have on agricultural production there.

---

Middle-level health teacher Maureen wanted to engage her students in thinking through some of the (often unintended) consequences of risky behavior. For example, as part of a unit on fetal development, she gave her students material from their text as well as newspaper accounts with information about environmental impacts on the fetus, including fetal alcohol syndrome. Maureen wrote on the board: "A woman who drinks during pregnancy should be detained. Agree or disagree and why."

Each student began by writing at least three to four sentences stating her or his position. She then asked pairs of students to exchange papers and comment on the other person's thoughts. After two more exchanges, students had pretty well clarified their own thinking and understood the position of their writing partners. To wrap up the activity for that day, Maureen put students into small groups of pros and cons and charged each group with summarizing their arguments in no more than six statements—thus requiring practice categorizing, summarizing, and synthesizing.

Maureen had other alternatives for building on this Written Conversation. After the initial exchanges, she might have asked students to circle an idea that was most potent for them individually and bring that idea to the class for discussion or further exploration. She could have worked with the social studies teacher to relate the topic to students' earlier study of the Constitution and individual rights and freedoms. She might also have assigned students to write a letter to the editor expressing their ideas or concerns and suggesting potential solutions.

Written Conversations can serve to build both rigor and stamina. Everyone has to write, so no student sits back and watches. Because the reader is a peer, the stakes are high; Grade 4–8 students in this situation generally try to write something of worth. Expanding the group from a pair to four or five students often requires greater attention to clarity, increasing the rigor of the writing in terms of needing to use appropriate vocabulary for the discipline, putting forth a cogent argument, and presenting that argument in a coherent way. This is a good activity for supporting the development of learning to think like a mathematician, social scientist, scientist, and so forth.

*After reading and discussing* An Angel for Solomon Singer, *Jolene asked all of her students to write in their learning logs to the prompt "Think about our conversation. What is staying in your mind? What might be bothering you? What is something you want* to think about some more?" She gave them a minute to write but extended the time when students asked for more time to express their thoughts.

When they had finished writing, each cluster of four students then switched notebooks four times, responding in writing to the comments in the notebook before them by adding, agreeing, disagreeing, and giving reasons. Following this Written Conversation, Jolene asked students in pairs to create a statement for the whole class to discuss. Each pair wrote their statement on a three-by-five card for a Pass the Hat activity (explained later in this chapter). Students became very deep in their thoughtfulness about the book, considering such topics as death, angels, and a debate about old men being creepy versus friendly and happy.

Students in the above vignette became so engaged with the book and the topic that they sought additional opportunities to write their thoughts and wanted to share their thinking with an audience beyond the classroom. Jolene could have then assigned an essay, poem, or letter to the editor, each with its own requirements for form and voice.

*Reflection and Action*

After using Written Conversation, what were your "*ahas*" as you watched/listened to your students work? What insights do you have about the process, about individual students, about the class? Did you notice if any of your students were using skills like analyzing, synthesizing, comparing, contrasting, or using evidence from a text to support a statement?

Drawing on what your students have experienced, now think about how you might extend their learning—revisiting the text to find evidence to support their thinking or to look at it from a different perspective (e.g., as a scientist or historian might). You might also ask students what questions are still in their minds that they and you should pursue further, either as a group or with differentiated assignments.

Like all of the activities suggested so far, a Written Conversation is to be used to reach deeper learning and higher-level thinking. As you use it over time, you and your students will get to more meaningful learning quicker. You might find that collecting and analyzing some sample Written Conversations will give you additional insights into where you need to lead your students next.

### Troubleshooting Written Conversation

**What if you do not think that students wrote enough?** The first thing to look at is the text. Does it lend itself to different interpretations or points of view? Also look at your writing prompt; was it one that would encourage students to get beyond the facts to the implications of those facts?

Rather than give students feedback that is focused on length, concentrate on encouraging students to take responsibility for their own thinking. More writing will follow. Reviewing and adapting some of the prompts from the envisionment-building guides (EBGs) in Chapter 3 or Appendix A may help push their thinking so that they have more to write.

> Two teachers in a special education classroom reported that a Written Conversation moved their most reluctant writer to write more. This student struggled to write in depth on any topic, and his classmates were sensitive to his difficulty. They asked him to explain what he had written, and he began to write more on the next rotation. Perhaps he was checking to see if anyone would really read what he had written; maybe he wanted to see if anyone would respond to him. Whatever phenomenon was in play, the teachers witnessed him writing more than they had seen him write ever before in the classroom.

Exceeding teacher expectations is a common occurrence when students realize that the conversation is truly theirs and is meant to help them clarify and articulate their own thinking.

***What if students need more support/scaffolding?*** If your students need more structure to start writing, you might initially give them a framework for a Written Conversation, such as that shown in Figure 2.1. Note that the blanks do not ask for concrete facts but for thinking and interpretation.

## SCAFFOLDS FOR PRODUCTIVE WHOLE CLASS DISCUSSIONS

Chapter 1 asked you to think mostly about the *process* of discussion, but the point of having productive discussions is to help students learn the content—and learn *how* to learn the content. That is where to turn next. The tools and activities introduced in this part of the chapter all use higher-order thinking skills; they will increase the extent to which your students contribute to academic discussions by

- getting beyond the concrete—the basic facts of the material—to analysis, interpretation, and other higher-order skills
- relating the text or topic being discussed to something they have learned earlier or in another class
- relating the topic or material to a situation outside of school/academic learning—to the news, to the community, to personal interests outside of school
- pushing their classmates' thinking to a higher level

The four instructional scaffolds introduced below—reader's marks, video viewing guide, Pass the Hat, and pairing texts—help students better engage with and comprehend their texts so they come to class better prepared to add productively to small group and whole class discussions.

In the [ name of science lab or experiment ] our hypothesis was

_____.

We were able to [ prove or disprove ] our hypothesis by

_____

_____

_____.

I think these results are important because _____

_____

_____.

Response 1: _____

Or

I think that during the Revolutionary War my family would have been [Patriots or Loyalists] because [ give at least 2 reasons ] _____

Response 1: _____

Or simply,

When I read/saw/heard this, I thought _____

Response 1: _____

**Figure 2.1. Sample Framework for a Written Conversation**

## Reader's Marks and Variations

You probably invented symbols or ways to annotate a text in college or graduate school, but there is no reason to make your students wait. Many researchers over many years have shown that good readers mark complex texts, and making this process overt will help students to more actively engage with their reading and improve comprehension.

A useful concept to keep in mind here is that readers take different orientations to making meaning depending on the nature of the text they are reading. Judith Langer describes these orientations as maintaining a point of reference and exploring horizons of possibilities.[7] Maintaining a point of reference means that readers are seeking to gain information about a topic in order to understand it. Alternatively, while exploring horizons of possibilities, readers' minds are moving in a more open way, raising questions and forming hunches about what the text is about, for example, finding the inferences.

Reading literary works generally calls for horizons-of-possibilities thinking and informational texts for point-of-reference thinking. Strong readers can switch back and forth between the two orientations, and teachers can guide students to do so by asking questions appropriate to the type of text and the purpose for reading it.

Reader's marks are an easy way for students to begin to connect with a text, and keeping the number of marks down allows students to internalize the marks without feeling overwhelmed. In introducing reader's marks, first decide which one or ones you might like to include.

The three marks in the sample are recommended for several reasons: Underlining or highlighting will help students identify what is important and gain insight to the significance of the material. To further help students determine what is important—something that many students find challenging—and to further help them focus while reading, ask them one question that gives them a purpose for reading (and underlining or highlighting). This purpose question is especially useful for guiding readers to read for information (point of reference) or raising questions or anticipating what will come next (exploring horizons of possibilities).

Similarly, circling vocabulary is a good mark to start with, as students are quick to recognize the terms they are unfamiliar with,

| | |
|---|---|
| _____ | **Underline** or **Highlight** the parts that you want to talk about, that remind you of something else, or that you think are important. |
| (Vocabulary) | **Circle** a new vocabulary word or a word whose meaning you are unsure of. |
| ? | Put a **question mark** in the margin when you don't understand. Better yet, write your own question in the margin! |

**Table 2.1. Sample Reader's Marks**

and like a quick brush stroke, a discussion clarifying an unfamiliar word is easily incorporated into a class discussion before the primary lesson begins. In addition, it can spotlight the particular vocabulary of your subject(s), and teaching academic vocabulary is likely high on your list of must-dos.

And the question mark encourages students to ask questions—about things they don't understand or that they'd like to explore further. These marks also give you insight into student thinking.

*Introducing Marks to Students*

There are several ways to introduce reader's marks. First, ask all of the students to use just a few simple marks like those in the sample (Table 2.1) and introduce them on a suitable short piece of material (chart, graph, quote, cartoon, map, diagram, math explanation or problem, etc.). Or substitute one or more that are more suitable for your subject area, such as, perhaps, *xxxxxxxxxx* for crossing out unnecessary information in mathematics. Also in mathematics, teachers may want to adapt the marks to include placing an *F* (for "find") next to the problem students are being asked to solve.[8]

You might also model their use on a text that you expect to be challenging for most students and give students a chance to practice with the guidance of you and their peers. (If the text is one on which students are not allowed to write, sticky notes may be substituted.) See Figure 2.2 for a student sample that includes a purpose question.

> You can model using reader's marks with two to three student partners or a colleague, if one is available. Decide which partner will read the first paragraph or page out loud while the others read silently, marking their papers. All of the students watch and read along silently, marking if they choose. At the end of the designated section, the modelers discuss their marks and why they made them.
>
> Switch roles so that someone else reads aloud and the others mark. You may want to give another two to three students a chance to model this time or stay with the same students. Again, the remaining students read along silently, marking if they choose. Again discuss the marks and the reasons for them. The same kind of modeling can be done with the video viewing guide (Table 2.2).
>
> By the third or fourth turn, most students should be comfortable attempting to use the marks or guide, and the fact that the modelers likely have slightly different suggestions for what is important should give all students the confidence to make their entries without stopping too much to fret about being "right." You could also model this yourself using a white board or SMART board, stopping to discuss your marks/entries and asking students to compare their own—in pairs or small groups.

Teaching the use of reader's marks is definitely not new! What is significant about including them here is their purpose. The increased need to deal with the staggering amount of information accessible today is reflected in the Common Core Standards' focus on reading informational texts. Using reader's marks helps students

- physically engage with a text, helping to keep them "minds on"
- read complex texts purposefully
- easily reengage with a text when you are ready to begin a discussion of it or build on it with a further assignment
- begin their analysis of a text
- develop the mental habits of independent learners

Use or develop symbols or notations that work for your specific discipline(s) and lesson goals and then use the marks students have made to start discussions.

*Video Viewing Guide*

Translating reader's marks to nonprint audio or visual materials is a little more challenging, because a video, DVD, or audio tape needs to be paused in order to give time for students to respond. However, here are some suggestions: In a video situation, give students a template for capturing their *thinking* (not just looking for facts; see Table 2.2 for an example). After every four to eight minutes, depending on the level of difficulty of the clip and the age and attention spans of your students, stop the video and have students note an important fact or ask a question or make a connection with something they already know from the information they have just heard or witnessed.

Doing this several times throughout the video allows students to process the information in a more bite-sized way than waiting until the end to ask, "What are you thinking about?" With their notes in hand, they now have captured their thinking and are more prepared to discuss it or write about it.

*Purposeful Engagement* 47

How did the framers of the Declaration view the role of government?

........We hold these truths to be self-evident, that all men are ? What about women? what about slaves?

created equal, that they are (endowed) by their Creator with

certain (unalienable) Rights, that among these are Life, Liberty

*Does this mean being happy is guaranteed?*

and the pursuit of Happiness. --That to secure these rights,

Governments are (instituted) among Men, (deriving) their just

powers from the consent of the governed, --That whenever

any Form of Government becomes destructive of these

ends, it is the Right of the People to alter or to (abolish) it, and ? Are the people more powerful than the government?

to (institute) new Government, laying its foundation on such

principles and organizing its powers in such form, as to them

shall seem most likely to effect their Safety and Happiness.

**Figure 2.2. Sample Reader's Marks**

*Debriefing Reader's Marks and/or the Video Viewing Guide with Students*

After the first time students have used reader's marks or a video viewing guide, ask them to discuss their individual marks or entries with a partner (Think-Pair-Share) or in a small group. Ask them

- to compare their marks/entries
- to discuss how the marks/entries helped them stay focused on and understand the text or video

Discuss their responses in the large group, observing your discussion guidelines and capturing what they say for all to see (e.g., on chart paper or white board). Either the purpose question you assigned for the reading/viewing or any of the column headings on

|  | Important facts you have learned so far | Questions you have so far, including unfamiliar words | Connections to what you learned/knew before |
|---|---|---|---|
| Stop 1 |  |  |  |
| Stop 2 |  |  |  |
| Stop 3 |  |  |  |
| Etc. |  |  |  |
| At the end | Underline the 2-3 facts above that you think are most important (or rewrite them below). | Underline or write below one question or term you would like to discuss. | For one connection listed above, write below how it relates to what you just learned from the video. |
|  |  |  |  |

**Table 2.2. Sample Template for a Video Viewing Guide**

the video viewing guide provide a good place to start a whole class discussion. For example, you might ask,

- What did you learn that you did not know before?
- Does anything in the text/video relate to something that we read or learned about earlier?
- Does anything in the text/video relate to something you already know, whether from school or outside of school?
- Does anything in the text/video contradict something you learned before?

Questions like these help students internalize their thinking process so that they can become independent learners. The discussions that ensue help solidify student learning of the content by requiring engaged reading/viewing that calls on higher-order skills like prioritizing and relating new knowledge to old. Because students have their thinking in front of them, more students should feel confident participating in the discussion—making their voices heard—in your classroom.

This approach should also enable you to spend less class time going over material that students already know and focus instead on what is most essential or that presents the most difficulty. Another benefit is that you can quickly check their papers to see if students have been interacting with the text or are engaged with the video.

As students gain experience using symbols and phrases to engage in reading/viewing texts, they will come to discussions better prepared to respond and analyze content. When marking becomes routine, you can add other reader's marks to increase student ability to refer to evidence, to question, and to reflect on the ideas under discussion. These are tools you should use over and over again until students adopt them as their own.

*Reflection and Action*

Now that you've tried a discussion using reader's marks or a video viewing guide, ask yourself,

- What did you notice—about your students' "marked" papers, their pair or small group discussions, their insights in the larger group discussion?
- What evidence, if any, do you see of enhanced engagement? Learning? Students' awareness of their own thinking and learning?

As you think about student learning, what particular skills do they need more practice with? How will you differentiate? If they are marking too much or too little, see "Troubleshooting" below. Take a look at your guiding or purpose questions to see if they are pushing beneath the surface of the text to get at bigger ideas. Also examine the texts themselves to be sure that they are worthy of scrutiny.

> Susan loves the story "The Gift of the Magi" and has found a way to make this classic holiday story accessible to her students by sharpening their reading skills using a variation on reader's marks. Following a reading of the entire story, she assigns each pair of students one page of the text and asks them to find the descriptive details about the setting and then make a drawing to show how that particular setting pushes the plot of the story forward.
>
> In pairs, the students set to work excavating the text and marking it, discussing not only what to represent but how to explain their choices when they present their drawing's role in the plot to their classmates. One year, for example, a pair of students chose to represent the sparseness of the room by drawing a bare-bulb lamp. Students practice inference, close

> reading, and speaking while learning more about plot and setting. When put in sequence, their drawings form a wordless picture book of the story.

## Troubleshooting Reader's Marks and Video Viewing Guide

**What if students underline or write down nearly everything?**
It is difficult for students to know what is "important." Giving students a guiding or purpose question or two (no more!) before they read or view helps them focus, especially at first, and eliminates overmarking. For videos, it is important for students to wait until a pause to do their writing, or they will miss some of the viewing—unless they are viewing on their own and in a format where they can "rewind."

You may need to make accommodations for students who need to stop the video more often, and/or you can teach students to jot just a word or two of notes to prompt a fuller statement of their thoughts at the pause.

**What if students made no marks or entries because they didn't think anything was important, saw no words they didn't know, found no connections, and nothing surprised them?** Start by looking at the material you asked them to read or view. Is it worth the effort to dissect it and think more deeply about it, or is it a "watered down" version or a textbook excerpt that may not challenge a reader to want to know more?

If the text/video seems worthy of discussion and struggle, then be sure to model how to use the marks before assigning them. Also, as students are working, circulate and ask, "Can you tell me what _____ means?" If the answer is incorrect, or if you receive no answer, encourage the student(s) to circle that word. Or read a section/show a clip and ask, "What seems important from that selection?" When students respond, talk about underlining the key words/writing the key phrases, not necessarily the entire sentence or passage.

You might also ask two pairs to combine into a group of four and share their marks/guides so that the students who found nothing to write might discover from a more successful pair what the process looks like and why it is important in helping their learning.

**Pass the Hat**

When you are confident that your students are getting the hang of interrogating texts, looking for the most important, relevant, and/or surprising information, introduce another effective discussion prompt. At the conclusion of a reading or video, ask students to look at their reader's marks or video viewing guide and see if there is a question they want to ask. Perhaps there is something they are wondering from having read/heard this information.

You can ask them to write the question on a card and pass a hat (or box) around the room to collect the cards. You then draw a card from the hat and read it aloud to begin a discussion of the material. In addition to surfacing students' genuine questions about the material, this activity serves multiple purposes:

- For some students, the anonymity of the questions removes their fear of revealing inadequate understanding, and they ask what they would never voice out loud.
- Students who tend to think nothing is important in a reading or viewing may find that their question prompted a valuable class discussion, and they look at the material with new eyes.
- Students will come to learn that asking probing questions that are meaty enough to engage their classmates in extended discussion requires more than a superficial reading or viewing.
- You can avoid discussing material students already understand and spend precious class time pushing into areas that need more explanation and that deepen knowledge and understanding.

If students ask questions that require more information in order to discuss it in depth, you can capture the questions and put them aside (in what you might call a "parking lot") for further exploration at a later time—for going beyond, as explained in Chapter 3. Honoring and displaying such questions can help your students see the curricular connections, the bigger picture that you are striving for.

You need not always pull every card out of the hat nor read every card you pull if it repeats an earlier question. But it is helpful following a Pass the Hat activity to ask students to reflect on the questions and the discussion that ensued and what kinds of questions generated the most discussion and learning. This reflection will help students to think about and analyze a reading on their own by asking themselves the same types of questions.

> Derek teaches social studies and regularly uses student questions to learn what his students are thinking so that he can shape instruction to meet their learning needs. After his classes had looked at the spread of fascism in Italy at the start of World War II, he asked students to write a question that expressed what they were now wondering about.
>
> The next day, one of his special education students was surprised to find *his* question on the board for all classes to do a Quick Write on before the day's formal instruction began. The student whose question was used couldn't believe his question was being tapped for all of Derek's classes to consider, but he had clearly raised a question worth consideration by all students. At a conference with the principal, the student's parents spoke about that experience and the positive impact that such a seemingly simple act could have in turning this boy's attitude and performance around.

## Pair Engaging and Complex Texts to Foster Critical Thinking

In any subject, one key to engaging students is to use a variety of materials that are in dialogue with one another. Introducing texts in different genres and formats helps students learn to integrate knowledge. For example, you might pair a reading of the standard textbook with a video clip, map, chart, table, diagram, photo, or cartoon. Your goal is to find material that gives students enough meaty content to think about while at the same providing materials that are accessible to students with a range of language skills. All materials should point toward the same big idea but approach it from different perspectives or in different formats.

Offering students different perspectives not only provides more content for them to think about and with but also invites different student voices into the discussion, provides more opportunities for students to understand the content and consider the questions being raised, and develops higher-order thinking skills.

In math, for example, you might introduce a concept by means of a picture book or a picture (e.g., of patterns). In science, health, careers, or technology, newsclips or short magazine articles about the topic you are studying work well. In social studies, consider the concept or era you are going to teach soon; is there a piece of art or short literary work or historical document that would introduce it (perhaps a photo of young factory workers paired with a reading about dangerous working conditions of the same era)?

In English language arts (ELA), think about the theme you wish to explore. Is there a piece of music to introduce the idea? A poem? Getting students to think across genres is engaging and fun as well as difficult. Ask yourself what the students have already read in your own class or another. Is there a way to create a bridge between that text and the new one? Providing opportunities for students to grapple with different perspectives helps them learn.

For ideas about excellent texts for young readers, you might check out the "Choice Reading Lists" section of the International Literacy Association's website (www.reading.org/Resources/Booklists.aspx). There you will find lists of award-winning books or books selected as outstanding by young readers and professionals. Titles include both fiction and nonfiction; the lists are annotated and go back several years.

> In addition to the science textbook's section on cells, Pat read the chapter "Cell" from Bill Bryson's popular *A Short History of Nearly Everything* with her intermediate-level students. She then asked what that short but engaging excerpt made them wonder. Their questions included, "What causes your cells to have you wear glasses?" "Are there any cells that remain in your body for your entire life?" "How do we get a genetic code?" "If we all started with one cell, why are we so different, even from our siblings?" "Where do the dead cells go?"
>
> These questions helped her determine what to build into future lessons so that she could address their questions, and the students themselves asked if they could go and try to learn the answers to some of their questions. The pairing of Bryson's entertaining—but accurate—perspective gave students an excellent way to synthesize all they had been studying about the cell, enriched their understanding, and made them want to learn more of this essential science content.

## SUMMARY

All of the activities suggested in this chapter focus on engaging students with the content using a variety of texts, as well as activities for getting students to effectively voice their thinking and questions. Activities are scaffolded to allow students to become comfortable as they learn to articulate thinking in writing or in conversation with other class members.

In introducing your students to these processes, and through repetition helping them to practice them, you will be giving them tools for independent learning and for life. Hopefully, the activities described in this chapter have opened your classroom to all voices and points of view and given you ideas about where to go next. To work more on developing the kinds of questions that push student thinking and learning to higher levels, turn to Chapter 3.

## NOTES

1. Teacher in the youth correctional facilities system of New York State at a Partnership for Literacy workshop, March 2010.

2. See, for example, the Common Core State Standards Initiative, p. 46.

3. Marlene Scardamalia, "Transforming Teaching and Learning through Technology: Which Way to the Revolution?" presentation, University at Albany, State University of New York, Albany, November 1, 2012.

4. The term *Journal Jot* implies that students should keep a learning journal for each class, and that is a recommended practice. However, if this is not yet part of your routine practice, don't delay getting started. Simply ask students to use any piece of paper or provide paper. A third or half sheet signals that you are not requiring an essay and may be less intimidating for reluctant writers than a full blank sheet.

5. This is called a wonder question and teachers find that asking it always works. There are no wrong answers to "What are you wondering?" It frees students to process and articulate their thinking. It can, of course, be used as a writing prompt, as it is here, or to begin a discussion.

6. See Dan King, "Drummer Boys: Creating Historical Fiction and Studying Historical Documents," *Middle Level Learning*, May/June 2010, 10-12, for a description of this activity.

7. Judith A. Langer, *Envisioning Knowledge: Building Literacy in the Academic Disciplines* (New York: Teachers College Press, 2011), 29.

8. Other potential options include placing a *C* beside a part where they find themselves making a personal connection, using an exclamation mark (!) to mark something that startles them, a *P* for a prediction (useful in science or in reading literature), or an *I* for a place where they find themselves making an inference. While never wanting to overwhelm students with as many as 8–10 marks all at once, after introducing a few initial marks, you may want to present others over a course of study.

*Chapter Three*

# Purposeful Talk

*A Framework for Facilitating Academic Discussions*

> *When a person asks a question, that person is halfway to thinking about an answer.*[1]

Questions and discussion are essential components of every classroom. Teachers use questions to check student understanding and push student thinking, and lively classroom discussions promote student engagement. Asking different levels of questions helps students consider multiple possibilities, make connections to other knowledge, create new ways to think about and use content, and develop the habit of becoming questioners themselves.

As suggested in Chapter 2, it is important to encourage every student to participate in academic discussions. The way teachers ask questions—and support student questioning—can help ensure that each student feels comfortable contributing to the classroom learning community.

Research has demonstrated the importance of questioning in the human quest for knowledge and the benefits of classroom questions and discussion on student achievement. Questioning is an essential element of student engagement and learning, and teachers move through a series of stages as they develop and refine their questioning and discussion skills. In other words, asking good questions takes practice.[2]

Questions you may have asked yourself might include,

- How do I ensure that my questions and discussion techniques consistently promote more conceptual understanding and increase students' problem-solving skills?
- How do I create a classroom environment in which students actively ask high-level questions and assume responsibility for the success of their own learning?
- Although I know the overall goal I am aiming for, what instructional strategies might I add to my repertoire in order to achieve it?

It is questions such as these that this chapter aims to help you answer by providing two things: first, a framework to support cognitive development by structuring classroom discussions using question prompts that foster higher-level thinking and encourage deep student learning, and second, an opportunity for you to practice using content provided, with guidance and a format for planning thought-provoking discussions in your classroom.

In addition to calling on some of the tools introduced in Chapter 2, this chapter adds an envisionment-building guide (EBG) and T-chart. It also demonstrates using these tools with an extended example from Karen's seventh-grade social studies classes. Additional illustrations from other grades and subjects are included in Appendix A.

*Karen's heterogeneous social studies class had completed units on Native Americans and European exploration of other continents. The next topic students were to examine was the contact between European explorers and people native to the Americas. Karen felt it was important to examine this topic from both points of view and give students opportunities to grapple with the consequences of the initial contact to both sides.*

*She first assigned the excerpt from Columbus's journal included in their textbook.*[3] *In it, Columbus described his initial contact with the Taino people who inhabited the Antilles islands. This primary resource clearly presented only one point of view. In order to present an opposing view and better engage students in considering the topic, Karen followed the text account with a literary work. She read aloud* Encounter, *a picture book story narrated by a Taino child who recounts the landing of Columbus and his men from the child's perspective. Students were immediately pulled into the story and made the connection to the textbook version of the same event.*

*After reading* Encounter, *Karen began by asking, "What are you thinking? What questions come to mind?" These questions, which can be asked at any time about any content, immediately signal to students that their thinking is the focus of a discussion. The questions do not "test" for student knowledge or understanding; there are no "right" answers. Rather, the questions spotlight student thinking and open the discussion in a welcoming manner. Asking such open-ended questions is the first step in facilitating classroom discussions in which students become the "meaning makers."*[4]

## A GUIDE TO FACILITATING DISCUSSIONS THAT FOSTER HIGHER-LEVEL THINKING

When student thinking becomes the focus of classroom interactions, the role of the teacher shifts. It is still essential for you to ensure that the required content is taught, but in teaching that content you focus more on creating opportunities for students to make meaning out of the collection of facts. This is what is intended by the Common Core Standards' call for students to be able to apply their content knowledge. Or, as Judith Langer says, "Information counts but what students do with it creates knowledge."[5]

In other words, what and how students think about content is what matters. This shift does not in any way diminish the role of the classroom teacher, but it does require a change in voice and preparation. The teacher's voice shifts from testing for student understanding to also asking questions that push student thinking to higher levels by asking them to compare and contrast, summarize, synthesize, analyze, and/or evaluate. Another benefit of consistently asking such questions is that students internalize them and learn to ask them on their own, as called for in the Standards.

One way to achieve this shift is to center discussions on authentic questions, questions whose answers you do not already know because you can't know what your students are thinking. An authentic question invites students to contribute substantially to the flow of discussion through responses that you can build upon.

An inauthentic question, sometimes called a test question, allows students no control over the direction of the discussion. For example, a health teacher asking, "Why do you *think* it is important to exercise?" requires students to evaluate and synthesize information from their text at the same time that it invites them into a discussion. Asking "Why is it important to exercise?" might seem authentic, but it invites a recitation of information from the text without initiating further thinking or exploration.

Ideally, a teacher directs classroom conversation so that students can wonder, make connections, seek clarification, consider multiple points of view, and make sense out of the assigned material.

## The Envisionment-Building Guide

Preparing for a classroom discussion focused on student thinking means that instead of making a list of comprehension questions, a teacher adopts a questioning format that focuses on levels of cognition. Preparation for such a discussion involves developing an envisionment-building guide, or EBG, provided later in this chapter.

The term comes from Langer's characterization of knowledge development as "envisionment building"; by *envisionment* she means what is going on in people's heads at any particular time as they process information from any source, whether literary (a book, play, movie) or informational (textbooks, trade books, documentary film), whether approaching text with a horizons-of-possibilities or a point-of-reference attitude.[6]

An EBG establishes guideposts to ensure that the discussion leader (you) engages students in examining a topic from many perspectives and at many levels of thinking. Each of five thinking stances, described below, helps students examine a topic from a different cognitive level, from initial understanding of the topic to using it to create new knowledge. Creating the guide before the discussion is essential and enables teachers to ensure that high levels of thinking are achieved. Questions within each stance are designed to force students to keep moving intellectually.

The five stances as taken from Langer are

1. stepping into a text
2. exploring a text
3. stepping back and rethinking what you know
4. stepping back and objectifying the experience
5. going beyond by generating new connections or knowledge[7]

The rest of this section provides detailed descriptions of each stance with illustrations from the *Encounter* example from Karen's classroom.

## Stepping into a Text

Although the human mind does not move through the stances in linear fashion, the first stance generally is to step into a topic in order to establish initial understanding of a text or content. Teachers can encourage students to "get their heads into" the material by simply asking, as Karen did, "What are you thinking?" or "What questions come to mind?" Other questions that work are "What puzzles you?" "What are you wondering about?" "What questions do you think we might discuss?" This is where a discussion focused on student thinking begins.

Does it not make sense to initiate a conversation by asking students what concerns them rather than starting with what you think their concerns are? Asking questions like those above allows each student to begin to make sense of a topic while listening to and commenting on questions raised by their peers.

*During the* Encounter *discussion, when Karen asked, "What questions come to mind?" students responded with questions like,*

> *"Why didn't the elders listen to the child?"*
> *"Why did they think the men came from the sky?"*
> *"Why did the men steal from the native people after they were so welcomed?"*
> *"Did this really happen?"*

Students' questions were prompted by both the narrative and the illustrations in the picture book. It was obvious that they had connected with the text and were engaged in thinking about the event. Students were immediately questioning the validity of the event, a characteristic of thinking like social scientists.

Teachers who start discussions with open-ended questions (and then use an EBG to push student thinking to other stances) always come to the same conclusion, no matter how reluctant they were to take the initial step: student questions are insightful and reflect good thinking. They have come to trust that students are capable of sound thinking and that they will question and challenge in appropriate ways.

It is easy to get sidetracked by concerns about reading ability or lack of background information or ability to write well or whether students can make the leap to analyze and synthesize. But beginning a discussion with student questions and comments helps teachers to know what students are thinking.

Many times over teachers report that the quality and range of student questions grow as they become comfortable with discussions focused on making meaning rather than only reviewing content. In other words, when students are asking questions, they are minds on and engaged; they are "halfway to thinking about an answer," as suggested in the quotation that opens this chapter.

## Exploring a Text

Questions in this stance help students to develop a deeper understanding of the material and explore multiple perspectives. Questions should foster "crawling around" in the text to ensure understanding. Specific quotes and phrases of the text can be referenced in the questions you ask, as well as in student questions and responses. Encourage students to use personal knowledge as well as the text to make connections and explore the topic more deeply.

It is important that you prompt students to refer to the text in order to support conclusions or to give examples of their thinking, as appropriate to the subject. Requiring references to the text often brings more students into the discussion and avoids getting just one answer.

If you encourage students to listen carefully to what their classmates say, they begin to build upon a previous response or idea, adding more evidence from the text in question or bringing in additional knowledge. With practice, they begin to use a piece of the previous comment within a new question or comment, especially when they have learned the vocabulary for doing so (e.g., "I'd like to piggyback on that idea").

*In Karen's EBG for* Encounter, *she prepared the following questions to help students more fully understand the Taino perspective:*

- *What was the encounter like from the European point of view? From the Taino child's point of view? From the Taino adults' point of view? Use the text to support your response.*
- *How did the encounter with Europeans change life for the Taino? How do you know?*
- *What do you think the narrator meant when he said, "So I drew back from the feast, which is not what one should do, and I watched how the sky strangers touched our golden nose rings and our golden armbands but not the flesh of our faces or arms. I watched their chief smile. It was the serpent's smile—no lips and all teeth."*
- *Should the explorers be punished for what they did? Why or why not?*

In response to Karen's prompts, students referenced the story to illustrate the different viewpoints of the encounter and the changes it brought. They were especially drawn to the child's interpretation of events and discussed how it was different from that of the adults.

One student commented that the child knew the Europeans must be hiding something, and another responded, "What made you say that?" The first student explained that the visitors didn't make eye contact. Another student supported that conclusion and added that the visitors seemed only interested in what the people had instead of the people and their kindnesses. Many also raised questions about how this account was similar to and different from the account of contact presented in Columbus's journal.

The questions in this stance should help students clear up any confusion they may have about the material being studied and encourage a deeper look at the content. The material could be a text or trade book and/or an article or poem, a collection of data, a series of activities around a specific topic, a video, picture, graphic organizer, or any other audio or visual material.

Discussions become richer as students bring in background knowledge, previous experiences with the content, and connections they make with other examples. As Karen did in pairing a fictional narrative with a primary source, teachers find that pairing more than one text ensures an insightful discussion. Referring to Columbus's journal entries describing the same event enhanced the discussion of *Encounter*, and vice versa.

## Stepping Back and Rethinking What You Know

Unlike the first two stances, this one asks students to step out of the text they have been so immersed in. Now you prompt them to use the new knowledge gained from the material and discussion to rethink or reconsider their own prior knowledge. Has the text and discussion changed what they know about the topic? How has the text changed their thinking about the topic? Has it made them think differently about their own lives and the world they live in? Especially at first, you will need to provide prompts in order to help students learn how to step back and examine a topic this critically.

*Karen's* Encounter *questions that helped her students step away from the text to (re)consider their knowledge of the topic included,*

- *What point of view toward contact was author Yolen taking? What tells you that?*
- *How does what happened in this story make you feel differently about European contact with the Americas?*
- *How might the king of Spain have written this story?*
- *What did you learn about human life, history, or race relationships by reading this story? Explain.*

Students' responses to these questions reflected distaste for the treatment of the Taino by the European explorers. They referred to their knowledge of early cultures and expressed concern for the lack of respect shown by the explorers. They were able to compare and contrast the material presented by the two accounts of contact, and they cited examples from other events in history in which similar encounters occurred. Using the skills of social scientists and meaning makers, students actively took part in the discussion.

Especially when dealing with complex material or material that is a cognitive stretch for them, students will need to go back to the original text to further clarify their initial understanding. It is natural for them to need to do so, and as you listen to their discussion, you will know when to ask a question that sends them "back" into the text to explore it further in order to clarify or gain additional understanding before stepping out again. This will help them develop the strategies to independently analyze complex texts.

### *Stepping Back and Objectifying the Experience*

This stance continues to ask readers to step away from a text, but now they must objectively and critically analyze the effect the text has had on them as readers. This is one of the skills called for in the Common Core Standards; it is also essential in an age of self-publication and unmediated information available from the Internet, as well as for understanding the ways of knowing and doing that are particular to any discipline. To teach this kind of analysis, ask questions that require students to examine the writing or presentation itself.

For ELA teachers, this might mean examining the writer's craft. For other content area teachers, it may mean focusing on the validity of the material presented. Students do not usually ask questions in this stance without prompting, but the ability to do so is an essential skill within all content areas. Questions that support this stance also help develop students' abilities as budding writers, mathematicians, scientists, social scientists, artists, musicians, and so on. Here is where they can demonstrate their content literacy, their knowledge as "apprentices" in any of the disciplines.

*Karen's* Encounter *discussion included questions about both the writer's craft and the historian's need to verify the validity of the data. For example, she asked,*

- *What aspects of the author's craft work well to draw you in and keep you engaged in the story? Do any aspects of her writing make you uncomfortable? Explain.*
- *What images linger in your mind? Puzzle you? Bother you?*
- *Why do you think* Encounter *is the title? What other title might work? Why?*
- *Is this story historically accurate? How do you know?*
- *What sources did Yolen use?*
- *How is the story similar to Columbus's journal entry? How is it different?*

Student responses were detailed as they compared and contrasted the two texts. They were able to reexamine the primary historical text—Columbus's journal—through the eyes of a Taino child. Even though *Encounter* is a work of fiction, students were able to see that the encounter depicted is historically accurate. The picture book allowed the students to make an emotional connection and thus made the content more interesting and more likely to go into their long-term memories.

Stepping away from the text and examining how the author shaped it helps students become critical readers. Questions should support students by asking specifically about ways the information was presented; what might be missing; the effect on the reader of images, including graphs and tables; how the vocabulary selected might influence an audience's reaction; and so on. Questions in this stance help students become proficient in reading complex texts independently in a variety of content areas.

## Going Beyond

The last stance becomes possible as students develop deeper knowledge and understanding of content. Here you ask them to leave the topic or unit and use what they have learned to go beyond to larger themes or concepts within the field, to begin to think of and develop new concepts.

This stance and the prior one (Stepping Back and Objectifying the Experience) highlight a major shift for students but help them meet the literacy requirements of the Common Core Standards. Literacy within each content area encompasses specific approaches to building knowledge and applying it in ways appropriate to that field. These two stances ask students to demonstrate their ability to think like social scientists, scientists, mathematicians, and so on.

*To support the thinking called for in this stance, Karen included such questions as,*

- *How is the event reported here important for historians?*
- *How are the ideas we've been discussing evident in the world today?*
- *What questions does the concept of "encounter" raise for you as a social scientist?*

Students discussed the importance of contact between American Natives and Europeans and contrasted it with other examples they already knew about—Alexander the Great adopting Greek practices, Europeans forcing changes on Kalahari Bushmen. They questioned the ethics of not just this encounter but encounters in general. Their comments reflected not only their ability to synthesize what they knew, but also their competence in generating new questions to investigate questions appropriate to the field of social studies, demonstrating exactly the kinds of knowledge and skills envisioned by the Standards.

By paying attention to the Going Beyond stance, teachers are able to help students conceptualize connections and themes within their field(s). For example, the contact between different cultures is a recurring theme in history. Revisiting the theme allows you to consider questions and engage students in the *work* of the discipline rather than rehashing the content. This stance also allows you to capitalize on student interests that indeed may go beyond the topic at hand. Rather than dismiss those ideas or questions, you can honor and support them.

Furthermore, students are not "done" at the end of any discussion. It is not even always necessary to reach a conclusion or consensus. In fact, the most successful classes are those in which students leave still talking about the topic or have to be reconvened to switch to another subject. One way for you to signal a stop to a discussion is to ask, "What are you thinking now?" "What questions do you still have?" Asking students to commit those thoughts to writing (e.g., in a Journal Jot) preserves them for future examination and discussion and can guide you in planning where to go next as you seek to meet your overall learning goals for your students.

Developing and using EBGs will enable you to steer classroom conversations that lead to "generative learning,"[8] learning that occurs when students go beyond the recitation of facts to generating knowledge and using content in new ways—exactly what the Standards call for. This stance is one of the keys to helping students make connections to the bigger ideas that guide your curriculum and instruction.

## A Teacher's Role during Discussion

A discussion guided by an EBG is not linear. Effective discussion leaders do not move through the stances in a prescribed order. Rather they move the discussion back and forth through the stances as students try to build understanding and knowledge. You don't have to ask every question on the guide you prepare, but you do have to ensure that the discussion hits each stance. If the material or topic is engaging, students will raise questions that demonstrate higher-level thinking, but the best place to start is always with a variation of the question "What are you wondering?"

As for what should be going on in your mind while a discussion is taking place—no matter how engaged your students are, your role is still key to ensuring that the conversation is meaningful and moves to address all the stances. In reflecting on her role in facilitating the *Encounter* discussion, Karen reported that she found that it required intense listening and assessing at the same time:

> It was much like conducting an orchestra, knowing when to bring the next section in, making the music rich and at the same time moving it along. I had to invite students into the discussion, listen to responses, encourage thinking and referencing the text, and at the same time ensure that each of the stances was addressed. I had to decide when to step in to encourage elaboration or clarification or when to highlight a student response for consideration by the rest of the class. I had to decide when the conversation had stalled or lost focus and move it forward with a question from my prepared EBG.
>
> Although the role of facilitator seemed large, I felt my role with an envisionment-building guide in hand was more defined than it had been in previous class discussions. With the EBG, I had a clear idea of where the conversation was going and how to move it there. Using the stances of the guide to structure the conversation helped me ensure that students were grappling with understanding the course materials as well as developing higher-level thinking skills and practicing the ways of thinking and knowing of social scientists.

As classroom teachers and as teacher coaches, the authors' experiences with the stances and EBGs have been extremely positive. Classroom discussions become thoughtful and engaging and often spill out into the hallways after class. As students become comfortable with the format, they begin to respond to each other with supportive comments and challenging questions. Conversations unfold with the teacher occasionally stepping in as facilitator with a question to explore a different stance, but no longer are eyes looking only to the teacher for affirmation.

The EBG helps teachers frame the discussion so that they push student thinking and explore content deeply. This does not happen overnight, neither for Johanna nor Karen as they were learning the process nor for the teachers they have worked with since. It requires practice to create an EBG that hits each stance and practice facilitating discussions using the guide to encourage students to think critically.

Working with other teachers to become familiar with the stances and to develop guides is very helpful, and it is important to find partners for this work whenever and wherever you can. Inviting a peer into your classroom to observe a discussion and provide feedback is also an effective way for you to develop your skill in this powerful instructional strategy. But please don't let these cautions prevent you from trying.

The next section offers an opportunity for you to try your hand at writing an EBG for a poem and then guides you through writing and trying an EBG in one of your classes.

## PREPARING FOR AND FACILITATING DISCUSSIONS THAT FOSTER HIGHER LEVELS OF THINKING

*Roberto had a good rapport with his fourth-grade students and often read aloud chapter books for their enjoyment. When he learned about and experienced envisionment-building discussions, he decided to give them a try. He took baby steps at first, simply asking, "What do you think?" at the conclusion of a reading. Then he ventured further with, "How do you think Grandma felt at the end of the story?" (*Stand Tall, Molly Lou Melon*).*

*His students were not used to this kind of question, which was asking them to explore the story in a bit more depth and relate it to other things they knew, so they had little to say. Rather than give up, Roberto tried again. Then he added writing. After reading* Among the Brave, *the third in a series by Margaret Peterson Haddix, he asked students to write about the two previous titles in the series. The writing gave students more to talk about, and he found their discussions richer for it.*

*After he had been building their discussion and writing skills for several months, he led a discussion of* The Toll Bridge Troll. *First, he showed the students a black-and-white illustration from the text and asked what the picture made them think: "What comes to your mind?" Students wrote for 10–15 minutes, all 20 of them thoroughly engaged. When it was time to stop, one student asked if they would now read the book; they expected to connect writing, reading, and thinking.*

*First, though, Roberto asked, "How did the picture make you feel?" Buoyed by their writing, students responded from various cognitive stances. One said, "I would run away if I was the boy and found a troll." Another compared the picture to* Midnight Magic, *a text read the week prior, comparing the witch to the troll and the castle to the bridge.*

*As skilled as he was becoming at facilitating thought-provoking discussions, Roberto still made an EBG in advance, but he didn't have to ask as many of his questions because students were internalizing the stances and were beginning to ask and answer questions at higher cognitive levels—for example, comparing and contrasting or considering the writer's craft.*

Like Roberto in the vignette, teachers who have made the switch to using EBGs to facilitate discussions never turn back. That does not mean that they have such discussions every day, but they use them when they want to capture students' interest when introducing a new topic of study, engage them deeply in a topic, or help them synthesize information across several days of work. Once you get the hang of it, you'll have no trouble deciding when such discussions are most appropriate—likely with the same material you now plan discussions for.

## Practicing with a Well-Known Poem

The poem engraved on the base of the Statue of Liberty offers an opportunity to practice writing and using an EBG. In addition to its literary value, the poem can also be used as an informational text, lending itself to both point-of-reference and horizons-of-possibilities reading.

Read through the poem reprinted below. After two or three readings, try your hand at drafting an EBG, following the guidance provided. The purpose of your questions is to structure a potential discussion whose participants—your students or adult colleagues—would consider the poem from each of the stances. This exercise will be more rewarding if you do it with a colleague or colleagues.

### *The New Colossus*
#### *Emma Lazarus*

Not like the brazen giant of Greek fame,
With conquering limbs astride from land to land;
Here at our sea-washed, sunset gates shall stand
A mighty woman with a torch, whose flame
Is the imprisoned lightning, and her name
Mother of Exiles. From her beacon-hand
Glows world-wide welcome; her mild eyes command
The air-bridged harbor that twin cities frame.
"Keep, ancient lands, your storied pomp!" cries she
With silent lips. "Give me your tired, your poor,
Your huddled masses yearning to breathe free,
The wretched refuse of your teeming shore.
Send these, the homeless, tempest-tost to me,
I lift my lamp beside the golden door!"

## How to Develop an Envisionment-Building Guide

*Stepping into a Text*

Questions to help students use their background knowledge and experience to approach a new text or return to it when they become confused. They begin to connect new concepts to make a mental picture of the topic.

*Exploring the Text*

Questions to help students explore and clarify understanding; the goal is to make sure students understand the content and connect relevant details to build a more cohesive understanding of the specific topic.

*Stepping Back and Rethinking What You Know*

Questions to help students "step out" of the text and connect it to other activities, knowledge, and/or events. Ask students to think about what they are learning from the text to help them better understand the larger topic.

*Stepping Back and Objectifying the Experience*

Questions to help students critically and objectively examine the craft and structure of the text; probes might ask about its authenticity, sources, accuracy, soundness of reasoning and/or structure, and what effect each has on the reader/listener/viewer.

*Going Beyond*

Questions to help students use what they have learned and discussed to further explain, clarify, or explore larger themes or concepts within the field.

The EBG that follows includes some sample questions for an EBG for "The New Colossus." Remember, many questions can be written to fit each stance. What is important is that the guide serve as a tool for a discussion leader; it is a visual reminder to prompt each kind of thinking within the discussion, and prepared questions can be used if student comments do not get to all of the cognitive stances. The third through fifth stances are especially important to prepare for because most students initially will not ask questions or make comments that reflect these higher-order thinking skills.

\* \* \*

## Sample Envisionment-Building Guide for "The New Colossus"

*Stepping into a Text*

- What are your first impressions?
- What questions come to mind after reading the poem?

*Exploring the Text*

- What do you think of the ending of the poem?
- How does it relate to the beginning?
- What does Lazarus mean when she writes, "'Keep, ancient lands, your storied pomp!' cries she with silent lips?"
- What conclusions about immigration or immigrants can you draw from the poem?

*Stepping Back and Rethinking What You Know*

- Does the poem cause you to think differently about the label "illegal alien"? If so, how? Why?
- What are you learning about history by reading the poem?

## Stepping Back and Objectifying the Experience

- What parts of the text—phrases, sentences, or images—were especially powerful for you? Why?
- Is the title of the poem appropriate? If not, what would you suggest instead?
- How was gathering information from the poem different from gathering information from other types of texts?

## Going Beyond

- How does the Lazarus poem relate to immigration today? In the past?
- What questions does this poem raise for a social scientist?
- Can you think of another literary piece with the same theme? What is it?
- Think about [name another country]. What main idea do you think describes it?

## Reflection and Action

After you have compared the two EBGs for "The New Colossus," your own and the sample provided, consider the following:

- How did your questions compare; in what ways were they similar or different?
- How would you now change any of the questions you wrote if you were to use this poem with students?

\* \* \*

In reflecting on this exercise and preparing to develop an EBG with material for your own classroom, remember to think about the importance of authentic questions. It helps to use a blank with prompts such as that provided above. (You will also find samples of EBGs and other tools for a variety of subjects in Appendix A.)

Those learning about EBGs inevitably raise questions about what should be included in a particular stance, and some questions might fit more than one stance. Don't stress out about being "right." It is more important to think about the goal of achieving a class discussion in which students engage in meaning making and that encourages and supports high levels of thinking. As you become more comfortable with the process, creating EBGs becomes much easier.

## Trying an EBG and Discussion in Your Classroom

This book always encourages you to take small steps toward change while keeping one foot grounded in the familiar. Asking you to try an envisionment-building discussion is probably the biggest leap recommended, and the first step may, indeed, feel like a leap with both feet. Please take that leap and trust that if you have been using the tools and activities introduced in Chapters 1 and 2, your students are ready and will not disappoint you.

Select material that will interest students and encourage discussion. It can be an excerpt from a text, a picture, painting, cartoon, video, primary source, quote, simulation, activity, or graphic organizer—or all the material in a unit you are reviewing. The options are endless, but the goal is to use material that will generate a thought-provoking discussion about important content. Sample lessons for science and mathematics, including EBGs and vignettes, are in Appendix A.

### Before the Discussion

Create your EBG by drafting questions that will address each stance. You may want to use the guide included above and/or refer to the sample for "The New Colossus." It will be helpful to work with a colleague to create the guide; this person need not be a peer teaching the same subject matter in order to be helpful in developing thoughtful and probing questions.

Have students experience or review your chosen text either in class or as homework in preparation for class; assigning reader's marks, video viewing guides, T-charts, or other graphic organizers to help them capture their thinking will help. Before beginning the discussion, arrange the classroom so that students can see one another and review with students the discussion guidelines. Then jump in! Start by asking, "What are you wondering?" "What are you thinking?" These initial questions always invite students into the conversation and signal that their responses are what will move the discussion forward.

## During the Discussion

What needs to be going on in your mind while the conversation is unfolding? As students discuss the text, it is important for you to listen to and monitor the conversation. Remember, you are not listening for "right" answers or for a consensus. As you listen and facilitate, you are essentially doing three things: (1) helping students to develop appropriate academic discussion skills, including addressing each other, not just you; (2) helping students to develop a rich understanding of the assigned material; and (3) guiding the conversation to produce higher-level thinking.

You need not ask every question on your guide, but you need to touch every stance in order for students to reach a rich understanding of the content. Student questions can also move the conversation to the higher-level stances. You are listening to ensure that each stance is approached so that all levels of thinking are addressed.

At first this role may seem overwhelming, and students may not demonstrate the level of thinking you would like. With practice, students will become more skilled in participating and in examining the texts in a deeper manner, and you will be able to get to all of the stances, which is important for developing the higher-order thinking you are striving for.

Also, at first your students will likely look to you for affirmation and support when they respond. Your task is to guide them to respond to each other. Some teachers have found that they can address this by trying to diagram the conversation and taking notes about who contributes; others have used a ball of yarn that students pass to the next speaker—a visual reminder that they are addressing each other as well as a physical (if entangled) record of who spoke.

When the conversation stalls or they seem stuck, jump in with a question. Depending on your assessment of their current thinking and understanding, you might say, "Can you show us the parts of the text that made you think that?" or "Does anyone want to build on that?" Questions like these will help "up the ante" to higher thinking and a richer understanding of the content.

Refer to your guide and mentally assess and check off whether or not each stance is being addressed by your questions and the student conversation. Remember that it may take some practice before you and your students feel comfortable with this format and you are completely satisfied with the flow and content of the discussion.

## After Discussion

It is important to leave time for you and your students to process what has taken place in terms of both content and conversation skills. Ask students what they thought about the conversation, by asking, for example,

- How many people participated?
- What could we do to encourage more people to share their thinking?
- Were people building on and connecting to each other's ideas and the text or simply stating opinions?

- How was this discussion different than previous discussions?

One or two of these questions might be the prompt for a Journal Jot followed by a Think-Pair-Share before being taken up by the whole class.

You may want to share your own observations with the class, saying, for example, "I noticed that several people referenced the text to make a point." "I was impressed with the thinking demonstrated." Teachers often find themselves without the time to reflect on what has developed in their classrooms, but it is important to include time for students to think about the process and talk about ways discussion can be improved. Such reflections will help to establish for students that their thinking and talk are the most important elements in your classroom and that they share responsibility for their learning community.

Also ask students to jot down the questions they still have at the end of a discussion by having them write a few sentences (a Journal Jot that some call a Ticket Out or Exit Ticket) to describe their thinking about the topic at that point in time. It is important to have an idea of what students understand at the end of a discussion. Use their thinking to plan where your instruction needs to go next.

Karen concluded the *Encounter* discussion by asking, "What questions come to mind about 'contact?'" "Do we have enough evidence to make a case that contact between Native Americans and Europeans was good or bad?" Students wrote their reactions to the prompts in a Quick Write/Ticket Out before leaving class.

Reading these Quick Writes, Karen saw that they were clearly concerned about the effect of contact and questioned whether or not there could be benefits to contact. Their responses helped structure the next activity, which included more nonfiction readings describing the benefits and drawbacks of contact for the Native Americans and Europeans. The concluding project required students to produce a written document that portrayed the effect of contact from the point of view of the Taino or from the Europeans, depending on which group they drew in a lottery.

## Reflection and Action

With student reflection comments in head and hand, consider the following questions:

- What did you notice about the student talk? About which students contributed?
- What did you notice about your use of the EBG? To what extent did the EBG help you achieve the goal of focusing the discussion and pushing higher-level thinking?
- How did this discussion compare to other class discussions you have held?
- With what material will you try this next?

---

**Karen's Reflections on Leading
Envisionment-Building Discussions**

My first attempts at facilitating a discussion using an EBG didn't always go as smoothly as I would have liked. But I did notice changes in student engagement and thinking, and this was enough to encourage me to continue. I worked with other teachers to create guides and share feedback on what was happening in our classrooms. Shifting my role so that discussion focused on student thinking rather than my questions required more from my students, and they began to accept more ownership for their own learning. These discussions really helped them to become independent learners.

    One of my early concerns was the issue of time. How could I possibly fit this much discussion in, considering the amount of content to be addressed over the course of the year? But the resulting engagement and thinking reflected by the students convinced me of the value of spending classroom time in this way. I was constantly impressed with the enthusiasm of my students. Humans of all ages—especially upper elementary and middle-level students—are social beings, and the use of student talk in the classroom definitely taps into this social need.

Student conversation that is focused on content and thinking about the content is engaging and made my classroom a vibrant place to be. It became the norm for students to ask questions, challenge each other, and think out loud in order to wrestle with the social studies content.

The EBG lassoed the conversation and kept it moving forward while stressing higher-level thinking skills. I felt that discussions were focused and meaningful. Allowing time for students to reflect on the discussions and their participation helped to develop their discussion skills. They became better at thinking like social scientists—adept at stating an opinion and providing the support to defend their point of view. This in turn led to stronger essay writing.

Over time, I got better at facilitating conversations, and student participation grew. Students became more skilled, and discussions required fewer prompts. I found that content knowledge grew as students wrestled to make connections and consider multiple points of view. Students clearly were working hard to make meaning from the materials and the discussions. Their responses helped to guide my instructional practice in a very effective way.

## Troubleshooting Envisionment-Building Discussions

**What if students are reluctant to participate?** As suggested in Chapter 2, asking students to write a Journal Jot/Quick Write before beginning a discussion gives them the opportunity to collect their thoughts and silently rehearse their possible contributions.

This rehearsal can help students who may be reluctant to participate otherwise. As you walk around the room, it can also help you see what students are thinking.

You may want to use Pass the Hat to be sure that all voices contribute to the discussion. The anonymity of Pass the Hat helps even the most unsure or risk-averse students realize that others in the class have similar thoughts. They also hear that others are approaching an issue or problem from a totally different viewpoint. Even more important, they come to understand that all points of view are valued and contribute to the learning of all. You are likely to find that with practice student questions begin to touch on all of the stances, and you will learn to use prompts to increase that probability.

Allowing time to debrief a discussion also helps classroom conversation to become more effective. You can ask, "How can we encourage others to participate?" "What can we do to make more of our classmates comfortable about expressing their points of view?" Questions like these make it the responsibility of all of the members of the group to work on this, not just you.

Students are perceptive about the dynamic of classroom discussion and will contribute suggestions for how to bring more voices into the conversation. Although it is unrealistic to expect all students to participate in discussions with the same frequency or at the same level, providing opportunities for students to reflect on the process of the discussion can help them become responsible for high-quality discussions.

**What if students do not refer to content or text?** Again turning to one of the tools introduced earlier, assign reader's marks or a video viewing guide to focus student reading or viewing. Then prompt them to refer to their marks/entries as they contribute to the discussion. This will help them focus on the content without you constantly having to ask, "What part of the text makes you say that?"

Using a graphic organizer during the course of a discussion also helps students stick to the content and become effective participants. One effective organizer is a T-chart on which students record their thinking at various times before, during, and/or after the discussion. You can assign students to complete it individually or in pairs or small groups before a whole class discussion; you can also complete one on chart paper or white board as the discussion unfolds.

For example, one of Karen's preferred tools for fostering both metacognition and disciplinary ways of thinking is a multipart T-chart (see Table 3.1). Such charts are especially useful when using more than one source of information with contrasting approaches or points of view; the two sources give students more to think about by requiring them to contrast and compare. A horizontal line in one or both columns allows them to capture their thinking before a second reading or discussion and after.

Completing the chart helped Karen's students carry the discussion over the two days it took to deal with the encounter texts. Such charts also provide students a record of their developing thinking and learning.

For the T-chart in Table 3.1, Karen had first asked students to complete both columns after they had read just the textbook excerpt of Columbus's journal. In the first column, they were to describe Columbus's view of the encounter, and in the second, how the Taino viewed the initial contact, based on their reading of Columbus's journal.

After the read-aloud of *Encounter*, she asked them to draw the horizontal line in column 2 and write what they were then thinking about the Taino view of contact with Columbus and his men. Finally, students reflected on their thinking, as well as on questions raised during the discussion. Entries in Table 3.1 are representative of typical student entries.

Using a T-chart in this way helps students deal with both the material and their thoughts about the material and discussion. It scaffolds their note taking and allows them time to process their thinking, thus deepening their understanding of the larger themes/ideas to be developed. For more sample T-charts, see Appendix A.

***What if a student comes to class unprepared to discuss the text?*** Every teacher has faced this situation, and each teacher has learned to handle it in a variety of ways. Hopefully, if you have set

| Columbus's View of Contact (from Journal) | Taino's View of Contact (from Columbus's Journal) |
|---|---|
| friendly people | welcomed voyagers |
| puzzled they don't speak Arabic | swords of the strangers convinced them to do as the strangers wished |
| friends, came swimming to ships | wanted to please |
| brought parrot, cotton thread | helped Columbus get to Cuba |
| learned Spanish and also spoke a sign language | believed strangers came from heaven |
| kidnapped some as trophies of voyage | |
| will turn them into slaves | **Taino's View of Contact (from *Encounter*)** |
| | afraid of visitors |
| | pale skin; thought they came from the sky |
| | looked away as they met eyes |
| | focused on gold, not on people |
| **How did the text affect your thinking? What questions now come to mind? How did the discussion change your thinking about the contact between cultures?** ||
| The story clearly showed the point of view of the Taino, and Columbus' journal only the European. ||
| It made me think of the positive characteristics of other early people we've studied. ||
| How could cultures be so different in accepting others? Does this always happen? ||

**Table 3.1. T-Chart for European-Taino Contact with Sample Student Responses**

up a classroom learning community with your students, one of the rules you developed is the responsibility of coming to class prepared to discuss the work assigned. It is important to establish up front that every voice matters and that being prepared to participate is key for success in developing an understanding of the work.

At first you might want to present material to be discussed in class and give students time to read and react individually. Once students begin to value the discussions as important to their learning and thinking about the content, assign material to be discussed for homework, supported by reader's marks, a video viewing guide, or a T-chart to help them capture their thinking for reference in class. As a discussion unfolds, it will be obvious that those who did not complete the assignment cannot fully participate because they are unprepared (nor will they be able to complete a Journal Jot, T-chart, or Think-Pair-Share, which will be readily apparent to you).

If you choose materials that are engaging and thought provoking, discussion will be lively and students will want to contribute. Minds-on discussions become an incentive to prepare for class; students want to be able to participate in the discussion.[9] In effect, this approach is an example of how some teachers today have "flipped" instruction, reversing the common practice of explaining things in class and then sending students off to practice on their own for homework.

## SUMMARY

This chapter describes a process of using classroom discussions to promote higher-level thinking. The primary tool introduced is the EBG, a format to help teachers ensure that their questions support students to compare, contrast, critique, analyze, synthesize, and evaluate. Paired with the tools introduced earlier, as well as the T-chart introduced here, such discussions build literacy within content areas. In addition to the social studies example that provides a unifying thread throughout this chapter, examples for science, mathematics, and English language arts are included in Appendix A.

To readers who are asking themselves if taking the time to use student talk to build content literacy is worth it, be assured that many studies have shown the effectiveness of student talk in promoting learning and thinking in the classroom.[10]

As discussed further in Chapter 5, conversations within the disciplines promote a rich well of thought that cannot be accomplished by teacher lecturing or students reading in isolation. Discussion structured by Langer's cognitive stances ensures not only that students thoroughly understand the content in question but that they can use it in new situations.

Readers may already be thinking about how some of the questions in an EBG lend themselves to more than discussion. They do, indeed. Chapter 4 focuses on writing and on other meaningful assignments that can use the same framework.

## NOTES

1. Mikhail Bakhtin, *The Dialogic Imagination: Four Essays* (Austin: University of Texas Press, 1992).

2. Charlotte Danielson, *Enhancing Student Achievement: A Framework for School Improvement* (Alexandria, VA: Association for Supervision and Curriculum Development, 2002).

3. Joy Hakim, *A History of Us: The First Americans* (New York: Oxford University Press, 2009).

4. Although this example comes from Karen's classroom, her English language arts (ELA) and social studies colleagues, who were also working with Eija as coach, used the same materials and approach; all experienced more engaged students who worked together to better understand initial European-Taino contact.

5. Judith A. Langer, *Envisioning Knowledge: Building Literacy in the Academic Disciplines* (New York: Teachers College Press, 2011), 2.

6. Ibid.

7. Ibid.

8. Judith A. Langer, *Getting to Excellent: How to Create Better Schools* (New York: Teachers College Press, 2004).

9. An obvious advantage of this approach is that you can differentiate instruction by assigning materials of different reading levels on the same topic so that all students can productively contribute to the conversation.

10. E.g., Martin Nystrand et al., "Questions in Time: Investigating the Structure and Dynamics of Unfolding Classroom Discourse," *Discourse Processes* 35 (March–April 2003): 135–96.

*Chapter Four*

# Purposeful Experiences

*Assignments to Sustain Thinking and Learning*

> *In the act of writing, the writer externalizes his or her thoughts. The writer enters into a reflective and reflexive relationship with the written page, a relationship in which thoughts are bodied forth. It becomes difficult to say where thinking ends and writing begins, where the mind ends and the writing space begins. With any technique of writing—on stone or clay, papyrus or paper, and particularly on the computer screen—the writer comes to regard the mind itself as a writing space.*[1]

This chapter continues the push to get to the bigger/larger purposes of instruction by focusing on two practical matters: (1) clarifying thinking and making it public through writing and (2) developing meaningful, "culminating" activities to consolidate and sustain learning. Each of these topics involves much more than meets the eye.

Using writing to make thinking public serves several purposes, not the least of which is giving students authentic reasons to put their thoughts in writing. Yet writing to think is very much underused in U.S. classrooms.[2] Such writing need not always be polished (and graded), but it should help students capture and clarify their thinking. The sheer act of writing and sharing their writing with peers and, sometimes, returning to it later to reexamine or reconsider a topic, helps to build on and/or extend students' understanding.

The first part of this chapter suggests scaffolds—learning journals and an "open mind" diagram—so that through writing for themselves and with and to each other, students "cognitively collaborate." The ability to collaborate in this way is required in higher-level educational settings, as well as in today's—and likely tomorrow's—workplaces. Some scaffolds use old technologies like chart paper and white boards, and some use newer ones like SMART boards and other electronic writing/thinking spaces.

For assignments that effectively consolidate what students have learned in a particular unit or set of units, the challenge is to make those assignments more than a rehash of concepts and facts. Therefore, the second part of this chapter focuses on assignments that are purposeful in at least two ways—helping students consolidate their learning and thinking and sharing that thinking/learning with others. It provides guidance on making connections and pushing students to do something more with the material—to go beyond—doing the thinking and analyzing that not only secures what they have studied but may lead to new insights and questions.

## SOME TOOLS TO HELP STUDENTS CAPTURE THINKING IN WRITTEN FORM

In the passage that opens this chapter, Jay Bolter not only acknowledges the centrality of writing to thinking, but he does so in terms of today's writing technologies. It would be hard to overemphasize the role that writing, whether in words or symbols, on paper or electronic device, plays in engaging the mind.

The term *writing* here (and throughout this book) includes representing ideas not only through the written word but also in symbols, diagrams, graphic organizers, pictures, cartoons, and the like, as well as on paper or electronic media, including audio and visual media. What is important is the ability to capture and communicate thinking—to make it stable on the page, disk, "cloud," or next technological storage system—so that others, including its author(s), can respond to it.

Developing the ability to clearly represent their thinking provides an important way for students to demonstrate and document what they know. It is a desirable and productive habit of mind. In addition to being explicitly included in the Common Core Standards and seen as a requirement for many jobs, including virtually any professional position, writing/representing is an essential element of being literate in any disciplinary field and can support thinking (and thus learning).

Even teachers who do encourage and require students to write to think may not realize its power. Eija recalled a workshop she was conducting for teachers across disciplines where she mentioned the importance of writing across the curriculum. A math teacher, Jon, said regretfully that he didn't assign writing in his classroom. Having observed him teaching, Eija reminded him that he had students keep journals (learning logs) and that he sometimes asked them to write a Ticket Out. "You mean that's writing?" he asked. Yes, yes it is!

One reason she could say so enthusiastically to Jon that what he did counts as writing is that his prompts for those Tickets Out are thought provoking and require students to "think on paper." For example, "Write two to three sentences describing how you could measure the height of the tallest tree in the schoolyard."

Leslie, a special education teacher in a self-contained classroom, sometimes asks her students at the end of class to "draw a picture of what we learned today." If you have ever been asked to create an image to represent your thinking, you understand that doing so requires abstract, symbolic thinking—the kind of higher-order thinking skills the Common Core Standards are calling for.

## Why Writing Matters

In general, the more students write, the better they learn and retain information. For example, those who take notes do better than those who do not, short-answer responses work better than multiple choice, writing that requires analysis or reformulation is more effective than writing that asks simply for a retelling.

Perhaps most important, writing is most effective in supporting learning when writers—in this case, students—use it to reflect on current knowledge, confusions, and their learning process, that is, when it serves a metacognitive function. Writing that does not require such thinking but asks students to copy information from the board or fill in the blanks with factual material is really what Arthur Applebee and Judith Langer call "writing without composing."[3]

One group of researchers theorizes that a reason for writing's effectiveness in promoting thinking and learning is that when people are writing, they have to negotiate two things at once—the act of writing (whether with pen or keyboard) and what they know[4]—sort of a Socratic dialogue with themselves that keeps their minds engaged. If an assignment asks students to do something more with the information than retell it, so much the better in terms of students needing to use higher-order skills, generate new knowledge, and, thus, retain it.

Writing to capture thinking, for example, in Journal Jots or T-charts, is a "trying-to-figure-things-out" kind of writing. For such writing it is important that you allow students to use their everyday, expressive language—the natural kind of language that people use when exploring meaning, either orally and with others or individually in their internal musings—not formal academic language or the language of pieces written for the purpose of communicating with an audience beyond the classroom or to be assessed.

If you have opened up your classroom to student voice, you have also opened space for them to use their voices in writing. And if you have been having discussions like those described in Chapter

3, your students should have plenty to write about. The nice thing is that reading, talking, listening, and writing work together to build content knowledge and literacy skills.

## Learning Logs or Journals

One way to ensure that students do some writing in your subject every day and develop the habit of thinking on paper or electronic file is to require them to keep a learning log or journal. This can be a notebook or electronic folder that students use all year long. Or, especially if this tool is new for you, you might want to start with a single unit and provide students a small booklet or ask them to keep a single file using a computer or handheld device. The journals or logs should be available to students every day, so you may want to provide storage space in your classroom to be sure that students will have access to them.

Although you will be assigning specific Journal Jots and asking students to write to particular prompts, in order to develop the habit of writing to think, it is important to encourage students to write in their logs of their own volition—to capture things they want to remember or that they think are important. Let them use their own language—everyday language, whether English or another—as well as symbols and images, whatever works to help them capture their thinking for future reference.

*A middle-level science teacher dipped a toe into the waters of asking students to write every day by piloting learning logs with a unit on the systems of the body. Carla wanted to see if the journals would make a difference with the way her students understood the material. She chose her most challenging class for the pilot, one in which 75 percent of students were identified for special education services.*

*During the final minutes of each class, she asked these students to record their questions in their logs. They captured their observa-*

tions about the day's lab and reflected on what they were learning. Her question prompts included, for example, "What are four things you have learned about the body?" or "What are you wondering about after this lab/video/reading?"

The biggest surprise for Carla was that her students enjoyed using their journals. They began to feel as if they were truly scientists, recording their thoughts as they made their way through difficult material, even using the logs to prepare for tests. In reflecting with her students on the effectiveness of the journals, she learned that they found the learning logs more valuable than the more structured notebooks they had been keeping: their journals kept their questions and their wonderings in the forefront, helping each student focus on what she or he needed to concentrate on the most.

When she looked back over the year, Carla realized that "the journals were a very good and exciting tool." Not one child refused to keep a journal, and she decided she had found a new way of helping students who generally struggled to learn science. When she moved an assignment into a learning log entry, the learning became more immediate and more personal.

She was surprised at the depth of her students' thinking when she asked wonder questions about the systems of the body: "The students taught themselves that they can do science. . . . Every single one of my students is successful this year. . . . I was always pushing for deeper thinking, and the students were up for the challenge. They've all learned so much this year, more than any of the teachers on the team believed was possible in the beginning of the year."

This vignette illustrates how the learning log tool got students writing every day—building stamina. It also introduced the idea of being a scientist, of using writing and reflection on a lab experiment to capture and revisit thinking, changing or amplifying it if necessary. Teachers who use the learning journal/log find that students take more ownership for their learning, are more successful on local and state assessments, and are more engaged in the work of the classroom.

## Introducing Learning Logs to Your Students

If you have ever kept a journal, whether self-initiated or assigned in a course, consider what effect the journal (in whatever form—video, vacation photo album, sketchbook, audiotape, diary) has had on your ability to recall and share something that was important to you. Then consider how you might best provide a similarly meaningful experience for your students.

As always, it helps to work with a partner to help you think through whether you will try a learning journal for a unit or for the year and whether you will use it in one class as a pilot or for more than one class.

Together think about how best to use a learning log in your subject(s)—like Carla in science, to capture learning at the end of each day or lab; in music to write or draw images that come to mind when hearing a particular piece of music; in English to keep track of new vocabulary—whatever important content you want students to really focus on, think hard about, and keep in mind over the span of the unit or course.

Provide students a notebook, small booklet, or suitable material for them to keep during the time you have determined and simply ask them to record their thinking in response, at first, to Journal Jot questions or Quick Writes. You can gradually extend those assignments to longer assignments and encourage students to add their own thoughts and questions. Wonder questions are a good way to foster the latter.

Make it clear to students that these logs are a learning tool for *them*—they control what goes into them—but also let them know that you will occasionally collect, read, and respond to them so that they realize the logs are public.

*Reflection and Action*

After students have been writing in their logs for several days, collect them to get a sense of what they are writing. You are not reading for the purpose of grading their writing but to assess how effective your question prompts have been and to get a sense of students' understanding of the content you have been working with. You may want to simply skim all of the students' journals but carefully read the entries of a few key students as a representative sample. Some questions to consider:

- How well do the students seem to understand the topic?
- What questions do the students raise in their wonderings that indicate what you need to teach next or come back to?
- How else might you make use of a learning journal in this class or another?

**Open Mind**

Asking students to sometimes express their thinking in images or symbols can move them to higher levels of thinking because symbols are more abstract. An effective tool for supporting students to commit thinking to paper/white board in a variety of representations is an open mind diagram. Because it is shaped like the human head, it automatically signals that you are concerned about *thinking*. It could be the thinking of a scientist or mathematician who made a breakthrough (e.g., Euclid, Archimedes, Isaac Newton, Nicolaus Copernicus, Galileo Galilei), a historical character (e.g., Alexander the Great, Charlemagne, Napoleon Bonaparte, Abraham Lincoln), or a literary character.

Or the focus could be on what your students are thinking, from coming up with what they already know about a topic to collecting all that they have come to know and understand after a lesson or unit of study. This visual aid offers students the opportunity to capture and share their thinking in words, pictures, symbols, and/or diagrams.

An open mind diagram is simply an outline drawing of a human head (Figure 4.1); you ask students to place their thoughts in the space within the lines—inside the head in the image. You might start with students using the tool individually and then have pairs, small groups, or the whole class combine their thinking in a composite drawing. All students in the intermediate and middle grades seem to like using this thinking tool, perhaps because of the freedom it offers in allowing different modes of written expression.

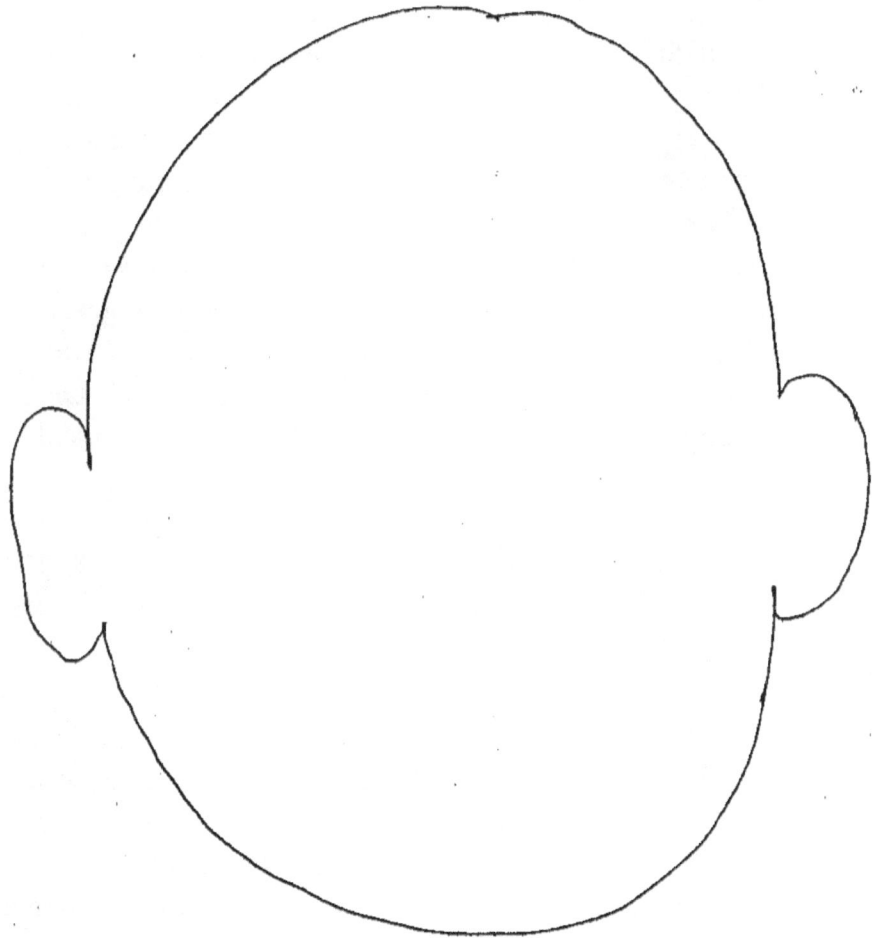

**Figure 4.1. Open Mind Diagram**

No matter how or when you use the open mind diagram, you can deepen student thinking by encouraging them to combine words in any language, pictures, and symbols and to think together. This is especially helpful for students who may struggle with writing or with English but who may be able to express their thinking or observations in symbols, images, or their native language. If you use the diagram to begin a topic or during the course of study, save what students produce so that they can return to it and add to it or change it; in the end, they then have a document that verifies overtly the thinking they have done in coming to understand the content.

> One way that April, a first-year special education teacher in a challenging urban setting, used the open mind with her students was to have them work in pairs to fill the head with adjectives that describe opposites, such as hot/cold, angry/happy, tall/short, and so on. Then in pairs, using *Lies and Other Tall Tales* as a model, students wrote hyperbole and illustrated each page they created. April then put these pages together into a book. Two sentences still resonate: "I knew a girl who was so skinny she used a fruit loop as a hula hoop" and "Oh, that's nothing, I knew a man who was so dumb that he worked in an M & M factory and was throwing out all the 'w's'."[a]
>
> [a]Janet I. Angelis et al., "Engaging Special Education Students in Higher Levels of Literacy," *Educator's Voice* 2 (2009): 2–13.

## Upping the Ante with the Open Mind Diagram

An open mind activity should include students sharing their thinking with each other and/or the entire class. Reporting out to the whole class is an important opportunity to deepen thinking and learning. Ask a question that does not let each group simply rehash what they did but that requires them to process the information in a slightly different way—to have to think at a different level or from a different perspective or cognitive stance—or to report what they think is most important about the topic (after a few minutes of discussion). Not only does this keep students on their toes, it gives them another opportunity to actively engage with the material.

After each group has reported out, you will want to assess whether they have covered the ground, so to speak, or whether you need to probe to see if their understanding is complete enough or whether you will need to fill a learning gap. Or whether it is time for an envisionment-building discussion that reaches all cognitive stances, sets them up for a more extended writing assignment, and/or reinforces the expectation that all students are accountable for the quality of their group's work.

During or after the final sharing, give each student or group time to add to their open mind diagrams to capture any new understandings, ideas, or information that they have gleaned from their classmates. At this point, each student should have a rich store of knowledge that can be used for a written assignment or to apply to another topic or relate to the curriculum's overarching idea.

The open mind diagram is a tool that in and of itself is powerful but when joined with others—wondering about a topic, capturing thoughts from discussions, writing from different perspectives—helps uncover big ideas that can connect a particular topic to all of the work a class is doing in a year. The conversations you facilitate around an open mind exercise are rich and worth the time and energy they take.

## Reflection and Action

Before completing your own reflection, ask your students to reflect on what this tool did for their understanding by asking questions such as,

- What did you notice about your learning and thinking during and after the activity?

- (For a new topic) What did the activity make you wonder about the topic?
- (For a review) How did the activity help you put together all that we have studied about this topic?

Feed their answers into your own reflection and what it showed you about your students' learning. For example,

- What would you do differently the next time you use this tool?
- How will you build on it?
- What other applications do you see it holds beside the one you just used?

> Leslie, a special education teacher, uses the open mind routinely to capture her students' thinking on chart paper, which she then posts on the classroom walls. She reports that doing so helps the discussion carry over from the original to subsequent classes.
>
> Students are eager to revisit their thinking and find more things to question and think about. One day, a student from another class came in and asked what the open mind diagram was, and the students themselves started explaining what they had done and the significance of their work on European exploration in the New World. Leslie was amazed at how much her students retained of their understanding and how well they were able to speak about the topic without any prompting or reminding on her part.
>
> Perhaps just as important, she reports, these students are the ones who used to try to hang out in the hall until the last seconds before the bell so that no one actually would see them enter this resource room. Now, proud of the thinking they are doing and can demonstrate, "That is all shifting."

*Troubleshooting the Open Mind*

**What happens if an open mind activity turns into more of an art project than a thinking project?** Please don't underestimate the power of a quick sketch to uncover some deeper meanings for students. Also, the ability to play with concepts in the realm of color/drawing/perspective will definitely help students uncover more about their learning than they had initially known. Before concluding that it's "just art," ask the student or group a few questions to probe the meaning of the representations. If the activity turns into embellishing the drawing rather than generating ideas, it may be that you are giving students too much time for the activity. Also look at the prompt. Are you giving them something with enough substance to think about?

## PURPOSEFUL ASSIGNMENTS THAT PROVIDE OPPORTUNITIES FOR STUDENTS TO SHARE THEIR THINKING

This book is a set of scaffolded activities designed to let you place one foot into the new while keeping one in the old—supporting you as you build new tools and activities into your repertoire so that they become part of your "routine" (although nothing about teaching is routine). For the most part, the instructional tools introduced thus far can be used separately or together to engage students in all aspects of literacy, including thinking.

This second part of the chapter adds some larger activities that are especially effective in helping students synthesize and share all that they have learned about an important curricular topic. Three of these activities—Gallery Walk/Poster Session, Carousel, and Stand and Deliver—are particularly useful in getting students to see the bigger picture, in tying together separate lessons into a more coherent unit, or relating multiple units to an overarching curricular idea.

You might be tempted to consider them culminating activities, but learning is never finished. So it is better to think of them as activities to use at points in your curriculum when you really want students to analyze and synthesize a chunk of material, review it, apply it, demonstrate their mastery of content, and put it into long-term memory. An added advantage is that all of these activities can be used as scaffolds to help students clarify their thinking before they tackle a formal piece of writing.

Unlike the writing-to-think activities introduced in the first part of this chapter, the formal writing introduced below requires that students use not only academic vocabulary but the writing conventions appropriate to a particular discipline. In practical terms, such disciplinary writing requires students to express their thinking as, for example, a scientist or mathematician would. Examples can include an essay, a lab report, a letter, or a mathematical proof. The writing process and format must be modeled or made overt by the teacher as the discipline area specialist.

The Standards call for students to be able to gather information from a variety of resources and use that information to support written analysis and reflection. The Standards do not deal much with the teaching of writing itself, and that is also an area beyond the scope of this book.

## Gallery Walk

A Gallery Walk is an activity in which students share work they have completed, generally in small groups. A Gallery Walk is distinguished from a Poster Session by the fact that in a true Gallery Walk, the individual or group that produced the work is not standing by their display to explain it. The groups that visit the work discuss it among themselves and make their comments in response to it in writing.

For a Gallery Walk, students generally record the results of their group work on chart paper, but it could be a laptop screen. Each group might have the same topic (e.g., explaining the digestive system) or you might assign each group a subtopic of the area you have been studying (e.g., one group explains the respiratory system, another the digestive system, etc.). The product of each group is then posted on the walls or displayed at the group's workspace.

Students move from display to display and observe and discuss the work of the other groups. Students can be asked to add questions and/or comments as they read the work of their peers; using sticky notes protects and respects the original work. If you have the technology for it and if your students are accustomed to using it, this process could be completed and shared electronically, then discussed. Following a Gallery Walk, it is important to do something more with it, for example, a whole class discussion and/or a writing assignment focused on what the students learned.

## Planning a Gallery Walk

Capturing and representing a group's thinking and communicating it so that others will understand it pushes students to reflect on the best way to represent their message. In turn, viewing a Gallery Walk calls upon students' reading/viewing/interpreting skills, as well as their abilities to conduct a meaning-making discussion in small groups. As Barbara does in the vignette below (also see "Scaffold for Viewing during/after a Gallery Walk," below), you must provide the prompts and scaffolds to help students effectively collaborate, categorize, prioritize, and identify key concepts. The hardest part is giving appropriate prompts that push students to higher-level thinking; the Gallery Walk is much more than a summarizing activity.

None of the required skills are simple nor necessarily available to students without scaffolding. Therefore, before you plan a Gallery Walk, think carefully about a topic that is important enough to spend the time on and that students will benefit from. A Gallery Walk does not need to be done often but rather when it is important to have students tackle a deeper understanding of important curricular content (e.g., a review of a unit or units) when they must synthesize and prioritize information.

In planning a Gallery Walk, some things to consider include

- Meaty topics you want students to understand thoroughly. These might be important concepts that are part of your curriculum and state standards and that students should know thoroughly before taking a state assessment. Of these, are there any that you can divide so that each small group has a meaningful subtopic with enough content to work with yet not too much to be able to share and explain in a poster-type format?
- A topic or topics that you have already studied that you are not sure your students have come to an adequate understanding of, yet the topic is foundational for future work.
- How you will organize students—in pairs or small groups.
- What scaffolding or tools students will need in order to prepare their material for the Gallery Walk. Will an open mind diagram help? A T-chart?
- How you will organize their sharing with the whole class. Will you place the onus on the written product (a Gallery Walk)? Or will your students need the extra support of being able to interact with the poster creators in a Poster Session (see the related box)?

*Scaffolding a Gallery Walk*

Encouraging students to use words, pictures, symbols, and/or images gives every student an opportunity to represent his or her thinking, even those who might have difficulty with any one way of representation. A mixed representation calls on higher-order thinking because the representations are more abstract and can increase the challenge for viewers to interpret what is written.

Since you are likely asking students to share thinking about material that the whole class has seen before, they should be able to interpret other groups' abstract representations. By asking students to represent and then process material in a new way, you are deepening their learning.

*During their reading of* The Giver, *Barbara asked her students, in groups of four, to develop a description of the government described in the novel. Each group used chart paper to provide a visual representation of how they understood the government to be organized. Since the students had been working in groups for several months and were familiar with representing their thinking in words as well as images, Barbara needed only to move from group to group, asking questions and pushing thinking, during this part of the task.*

*When each group completed the task, the poster was numbered and taped to a wall. Barbara had planned a Gallery Walk for students to learn from the posters of each group. Since the viewing was a new experience for them, she had prepared a guide for students to use as they moved from poster to poster. It included space for individual reflection as well as directions to focus their discussions about what they observed and learned from the other posters.*

As in the example from Barbara's class, in a true Gallery Walk students respond to their classmates' work by engaging with the product without the benefit of the creators being available to answer questions. Therefore, students need guidance in what they are expected to do, not only in creating the group product but also in responding to other groups' work. A sample scaffold for viewing during/after a Gallery Walk follows.

\* \* \*

## Scaffold for Viewing during/after a Gallery Walk

Part I. For each chart or poster that you visit,

A. **Individually**, jot down the most important or new understanding you see represented.

B. In your **small group**, discuss: Do you think something critical to this topic is missing? If so, what might that be?

Part II. When you have finished visiting and commenting on each of the charts, in your small group

A. Note **key words** or phrases that help to lock in your knowledge and understanding of this topic.

B. Discuss all your answers to Part I.B and decide on **one or two questions** or ideas to raise for the overall discussion in the class.

Part III. **Individually**, answer: What more have you learned about this topic from all that you have written and discussed? Be prepared to explain your responses.

\* \* \*

Taking into account your students' experience with this kind of activity, you first want to be sure that you know what you want your students to get out of it. That will help you figure out what kind of support they will need. You may want to adapt the scaffold for viewing for your students/situation. Consider, for example,

- Will students put sticky notes on the other groups' posters?

- Do students need guidance for taking notes as they learn from the other posters?
- What will you want students to do with the knowledge they gain from this activity?
- How will you extend their thinking?

The Gallery Walk can be a powerful tool to deepen learning and push higher-order thinking. It is essential to include an activity that requires students to pull together the content knowledge captured on the posters. A class discussion using an envisionment-building guide (see Chapter 3) can further consolidate knowledge and extend student thinking.

---

**Poster Session Variation**

A Poster Session, a variation on the Gallery Walk, is a little more complicated to organize in the classroom because the poster's creators are available to explain their work and answer questions about it. Depending on the space available and the number of students, you might ask three small groups to rotate from one poster to the next, giving time for discussion between viewers and explainers at each station. Again, though, students will likely need support to help explainers know what is important to share and viewers to know when to probe.

Especially if you are using technology, another way to handle the logistics is to have each group present to the whole class. After the presentation, the teacher or a group member could put the poster up on a wall or board to display with all the other presentations while the rest of the students are responding to the presentation using a guide such as that in the sample scaffold for viewing. Small group discussions might take place only after all of the posters have been presented and the students have individually reflected on them.

In Tony's class, for example, groups of students were each given a different character from *Because of Winn-Dixie*. They initially worked individually on an 8.5 x 11 sheet at their desks, filling an open mind diagram with drawings, words, and symbols that related to their character. They then met with students working on the same character and together compiled a more complete assortment of traits and feelings, using words, drawings, and so forth, on an enlarged open mind diagram on chart paper.

At that point, Tony hosted a Poster Session. He was delighted to learn that every group was ready to present their open minds and even more pleased as each group defended their choice of coloring, of omission or inclusion of particular details, and their interpretation of events in the story. Creators had gone back into the text to find and read the supporting evidence that gave them the close reading that he had been hoping they would eventually reach.

He kept their characters posted in the room so that each week they could return to them to provide updates as the characters evolved through the ensuing chapters. Finally, students wrote compare/contrast essays about two or more characters in the book using the discussions based around the open minds posters they had shared.

## Reflection and Action

As part of the whole class discussion following a Gallery Walk or Poster Session, ask students to reflect on whether and how the activity helped their learning. You might ask them to consider questions like the following in a Journal Jot and Think-Pair-Share, followed by a whole class discussion:

- What did you find most challenging and/or helpful about creating the poster?
- How did creating the poster help you learn more about _____?
- What did you find most challenging and/or helpful about learning from the posters created by others?
- What advice would you give future poster creators to help you better understand their message?

To guide your own reflection and future planning, consider what you have learned from your students, as well as the level of engagement of all students, especially those you might be most concerned about; what went well in terms of both process and product; what you would do differently next time; and where else in the curriculum you might use this activity.

## Troubleshooting a Gallery Walk/Poster Session

**What if students did not stay on task?** Modeling is always an effective way to introduce a new activity. If students are not yet comfortable working in a group, they need more practice with that before trying this activity. If they had difficulty cocreating a visual, have them practice in pairs or small groups using the open mind diagram.

Also look at the guide you provided them to see if it was clear enough. And remember, timing is important. It generally is wise to start by offering the minimum amount of time you think it will take, and you can always add another half minute or so, as needed. If it seems students are finished before the allotted time is up, begin the walk.

**What if the poster seems to be the work of only one student?** Some teachers give the participants in a group different colored markers, telling them they are to use the marker given them, which is an easy check to see if all students' thinking is represented.

***What if the information on the poster is erroneous?*** As you move around the room and monitor the groups at work creating their posters, you will see if the information that any group is conveying is off base or only partially represented. Then you can ask them to explain what they are creating and suggest that they refer to their notes and look at other material, including anything posted in the classroom from earlier discussions, that will help them draw more accurate information into their visual representation.

## Carousel

The Carousel is probably another activity you have participated in as a student or teacher. The basic idea is that small groups of learners move from station to station, interacting with the content at each station according to the directions given—commenting on what has been written by prior groups or adding new ideas. It can be used to brainstorm what is known about a new topic or, as here, to review or solidify an area of study. If you have participated in a Carousel activity, stop to reflect for a moment about what it was used for, how it worked, and what effect it had on your learning.

In the version presented here, you set up four to six stations with a different question, problem, or statement at each. The next step is to form small groups of students—as many groups as there are stations—and give each a colored marker, one color per group, with which to respond to the prompt. In the time allotted at each station, the group will need to come up with one statement, math sentence, or illustration to address the prompt. Encourage groups to have a different student do the writing at each station so that the responsibility is shared.

*To solidify her third-grade students' grasp of key concepts in mathematics, MaryAnn set up a Carousel with four stations: Addition, Commutative Property, Fewer, and Even. Her directions to her students were, "Explain using words, pictures, number sentences, or mathematical symbols [the term at the top of the chart]." She set up four groups, gave them each a marker, and assigned them one station at which to start.*

*In three to four minutes, each group had to come to agreement on one way to represent that concept. When time was up, she told the groups to rotate and do the same thing at the new station—but they had to represent the concept in a different way than the group before. She did this two more times, each time requiring a new way of representation. The "Even" station, for example, ended with*

> *8 x 4 = 32*
> *Even x even = even*
> *When you start with one, one is odd. The pattern is odd, even, odd, even...*
> *2, 4, 6, 8 are all even numbers*

*She concluded the lesson with a whole group discussion and student reflection on how the activity had served their learning.* [5]

MaryAnn upped the ante on student thinking by requiring that each group use a different way to represent the concept. Depending on the material, you may want to do the same, or you may want each group to react to what prior groups have written, adding comments, underlining what they agree with, and so on. This activity packs a lot of thinking into a short period of time, as the groups are allowed only a few minutes at each station, although the time may need to be lengthened in the later rounds to allow time to process what prior groups have written.

Once the rotation is complete, you can draw everyone together, share each sheet, and have everyone witness and discuss the synthesis of the entire class's thinking. An alternative is to ask the first or last group that visited each station to summarize the responses and highlight the key concepts, then open the floor for questions about that content. The Carousel's power comes from the way it pushes students into thinking more carefully and deliberately about content.

## Stand and Deliver

Stand and Deliver (also known as Four Corners) asks students to argue their understanding of a perspective on a particular topic and to try to convince their classmates to accept their ideas. It can be used to get students excited about a new topic, but it is especially useful for engaging students deeply in a topic and helping them figure out what the real issues are. In the sciences and social sciences, especially, many events or phenomena lend themselves to this treatment.

*During their study of monopolies, eighth-grade students arrived in Darryl's room to find this question on the board: "If it is illegal to have monopolies, could two people make secret agreements and make their own deals in business?" He asked students first in writing to strongly agree, agree, take a neutral stance, disagree, or strongly disagree. They wrote for a few minutes before he asked them to go to one of five areas in the room that he had numbered: 1= strongly disagree, 2 = disagree, 3 = neutral, 4 = agree, 5 = strongly agree.*

*Once there, members of each group shared what they had written and planned how to present their reasons to the other positions, with the goal of persuading others to come to their "corner." A 20-minute heated exchange ensued in which students shared their thoughts, switched their points of view, and then defended their shift. In presenting their arguments, they drew on information they had learned in class, as well as additional readings they had found on their own.*

*On another day, students found on their desks a copy of an article from a local newspaper that had identified their school as a "hotbed of crime." Darryl's instructions were simple and direct: "Read the article on your desk. Then take one of these positions and write your reasons for having this opinion:*

- *"I believe the article is accurate.*
- *"I have no opinion.*
- *"I disagree with the article."*

*Students read the article and wrote why they held a particular position. Darryl again followed the writing with a Stand and Deliver. For the next thirty minutes, the class, a majority of whom were identified for special education services, discussed their opinions, paying special attention to the language the reporter had used—a higher-level cognitive stance of stepping back and objectifying an experience.*

*Again, students were engaged, demonstrated close reading, and stated positions that were thoughtful and revealing. Students who had earlier been disengaged participated, and it was impossible from the level of thinking and engagement to identify which students were receiving extra support in the classroom.*

## Planning and Using a Stand and Deliver

Think of a topic that you want students to come to understand deeply and that lends itself to multiple perspectives. If possible, work with a colleague to craft at least one statement that, like Darryl's, requires students to argue a point. This is harder than you might think, and it will take time to develop and refine a worthy statement. (An alternative is to develop three to five positions on the same topic rather than a single statement with which students must agree, disagree, etc. This approach can be harder for you to develop but sometimes easier for students, especially initially.)

Once satisfied, decide how many positions you want to allow and if you want to include a neutral stance. Decide also how much time you want to spend on this activity. Be sure to give students time to individually think and respond to the prompts (e.g., in a Journal Jot) before they take their stand. You will likely need to allow a few minutes to explain the statement or statements, plus three to five minutes for the students' initial writing. Another few minutes are needed for students to conference before presenting their position to the others. The initial writing and conferencing are important skill builders and should not be skipped.

If you decide to allow a neutral position as one option, determine how you will engage and support the thinking of students who choose that position (more on this below). Also decide if you will allow students to challenge what they hear after each presentation or if they must take notes and prepare an argument to use when it is their turn to speak.

Another decision is whether to allow position changing after each presentation. Also think about the follow-up activity. A Written Conversation or more formal piece of writing are both effective ways to expand and further develop the thinking prompted by a Stand and Deliver.

## Things to Consider during a Stand and Deliver

Since the arguments can get quite heated, before starting it is wise to remind students of the discussion guidelines that they have generated. It also is important to make clear the rules of engagement that you have decided on for this Stand and Deliver—whether they can question or challenge any group after its initial presentation, whether they must wait to include their rebuttal during their own presentation, or whether all groups will be given a chance to present before any discussion ensues. Encourage students to jot down ideas from the discussion that they would like to react to or feel strongly about.

Preparing an envisionment-building guide like the one provided here can help you guide a Stand and Deliver discussion. Questions such as those listed for each stance should help students develop deeper understanding of the topic and create connections between arguments while highlighting unique points of view.

\* \* \*

## Envisionment-Building Guide for a Stand and Deliver

*Stepping into a Text*

- Do you have a question or comment for this (or any) group?
- Is there anything you would like a group to clarify?
- For those of you who are unsure, what questions do you have that are making it difficult for you to take a position?
- What information do you need to be able to take a stand?

*Exploring a Text*

- Can you give an example from your experiences to support your point of view?
- Can you give a scenario to support your position?
- What reactions do you have for the opposing positions? Are any parts of their argument plausible?

*Stepping Back and Rethinking What You Know*

- What ideas of yours have changed because of comments by other groups?
- Which comments made you reconsider your stand? Why?
- Which of your ideas have held firm? Why?

*Stepping Back and Objectifying the Experience*

- How effective was this activity in generating thoughtful discussion? Explain your thinking.
- What arguments were especially powerful for you?
- What additional information might further your understanding?

*Going Beyond*

- How are the ideas discussed relevant to the world today?
- What other questions has this discussion raised for you?
- What implications does this experience have for further research or better understanding?

\* \* \*

It is especially important for all students to feel safe in taking and/or switching a position. If one group is small (especially if it contains only one student), stand near that group to give their position more "weight." Also important is to be sure that students are comfortable about switching positions—and what is expected from them when they do, for example, making a simple statement about why they have changed their minds, what or whose argument swayed them.

Especially at first, be sure to occasionally invite students to switch. As they become more accustomed to this activity, they will learn to switch without an overt signal from you. For the neutral group, if you have allowed it, you might ask, "What is preventing you from taking a stand? And what would the others have to tell you to get you to make a stand?" Thus, no students will escape needing to think about and articulate their thinking.

## Reflection and Action

Questions to encourage students to reflect on this activity include: What did you think? Did any of your opinions change or deepen? How? Why? Was something said that made you think differently?

For your own reflection, consider what students said about the activity, as well as

- whether your initial statement(s) offered enough contrast for students to really engage with the topic and how balanced the groups were,
- whether you would change the format (e.g., all presentations first or presentation-rebuttal-presentation-rebuttal, etc.),
- what you learned about your students' learning and if anything surprised you.

If the groups were unbalanced, perhaps the statement needed to be more controversial or nuanced, so look for additional opportunities where the material might be more suitable. If students were engaged and productive, how might you use the activity again? If you used it this time during or at the end of a unit, you might try it as an interest generator for a new unit, leading students to formulate questions they will want to explore.

## Troubleshooting Stand and Deliver

***What if only one or two students spoke for a group?*** When students holding the same position meet to discuss their reasons for taking that position, ask them to take notes as they state their individual arguments. Together they then prepare an argument to present to the larger group. You might ask each group to designate their initial spokesperson—or you might assign someone (e.g., the students with the green notecards). Or you might direct them to designate two to three initial spokespeople to ensure that the responsibility is shared. The purpose of the statements they prepare and deliver is to convince students from the other groups to join them, so it is likely that more than one student in each group will jump into the fray.

**Extended Writing**

Although narrative writing is an essential skill for students, the Standards also require that students be able to write arguments using logical reasoning, accurate evidence, and credible sources focused on discipline-specific content. Students must be able to demonstrate their ability to write like an apprentice in the discipline being studied.

Examples include essays, op-eds or letters to the editor, investigative reports, mathematics proofs, journal articles, or other genres that require formal and discipline-specific language. Such pieces ask students to demonstrate their understanding of a topic and prove a point of view and can serve to develop and highlight higher-order thinking. This type of writing usually occurs at the end of a unit of study after students have had many opportunities to investigate, discuss, and grapple with the ideas presented.

*To investigate the interconnected spheres of planet Earth—hydro-, geo-, atmo-, and biospheres—Melissa assigned one sphere to each of four groups and provided a variety of resources to each. Following their investigations, she had each group report their findings to the class. She then conducted a Stand and Deliver activity to encourage her students to consider different possibilities and arguments in order to determine which sphere is having the greatest impact on climate change.*

*Then she repeated her question as a writing prompt for a persuasive essay: "The National Science Foundation will give one million dollars to fund one project in the one sphere that will best reduce the impact of climate change on all of the spheres. Which one of the four interconnected spheres is worthy of receiving this federal support?"*

*Her question required students to carefully consider a body of material, weigh the evidence, and then write a persuasive essay as a scientist would, with the additional requirement of placing that science in the larger context of society and policy. The opportunity to argue the question in a Stand and Deliver before writing allowed students to try out their thinking ahead of time.*

Writing as a scientist is different from writing as a mathematician or social scientist; therefore, it is the teachers of each discipline who can best teach students how to write in that discipline. Doing so prepares students not only for future study in that area but also for the essays that will likely be on their next high-stakes test in that subject. Posing a question or problem as the basis for an essay signals that students must do more than recount the information they researched but instead must analyze and evaluate it.

Incorporating the planning as well as the revising stages of an extended piece of writing into class time offers the opportunity to provide scaffolds, including modeling the work of the discipline. This also allows you to get insight into student thinking before an entire piece is written, intervening if necessary to push thinking and reexplain or redirect.

It is important to make the writing process overt for students. For example, asking students to chart their thinking before beginning to write is one way to scaffold the writing and thinking process. One tool for this is a T-chart that details the arguments to be made and the evidence to support them; the chart provides a way for students to organize their thoughts.

A facilitated class discussion that grapples with the key ideas (e.g., in a Stand and Deliver) helps students to rehearse possible arguments and consider potential evidence. Using academic language in classroom talk will help ensure that it shows up in student writing. Providing opportunities to write notes before, during, and after a discussion provides additional data for later writing.

## Troubleshooting Extended Writing

**What if students did not respond to the prompt but simply listed information?** Students will not automatically know how to write in your discipline. You must explicitly teach them the format, ways of presenting evidence, ways of arguing, and the voice to use in your subject. This will take good modeling, clear expectations and rubrics, and lots of practice. Some scaffolds you might use include frame paragraphs, sentence starters, graphic organizers, and/or many of the activities and tools in the earlier chapters of this book. Another scaffold can be prewriting charts on which they list what they know on both sides of an argument and then write on the one they feel most comfortable defending.

**What if I have students who have extreme difficulty writing?** No matter their print literacy skills, all students can think. In addition to the suggestions above, encourage such students to use helpful technology. If they are classified, work with their special educators. Most of all, make writing a normal part of their daily classroom experience.

## SUMMARY

Activities such as those suggested in this chapter help to develop good thinking habits, build strong content knowledge, and require students to develop independence and work together and learn how to communicate for different purposes and audiences—some of the literacy skills demanded by the Common Core Standards. Scaffolds such as learning logs or journals and the open mind diagram support different learning styles while fostering independent writing and socially supported learning.

Activities like the Gallery Walk, Carousel, and Stand and Deliver are especially useful in order to help students consolidate knowledge and practice communicating their thinking and learning in ways that are appropriate to the subject they are studying. Extended writing pieces develop rigor and help students internalize writing skills specific to each content area.

## NOTES

1. Jay D. Bolter, *Writing Space: The Computer, Hypertext, and the History of Writing.* (Hillsdale, NJ: Lawrence Erlbaum Associates, 1991), 11.

2. Arthur N. Applebee and Judith A. Langer, *Writing Instruction That Works: Proven Methods for Middle and High School Classrooms* (New York: Teachers College Press, 2014).

3. Arthur N. Applebee and Judith A. Langer, "A Snapshot of Writing Instruction in Middle Schools and High Schools," *English Journal* 100, no. 6 (2011): 14–27.

4. Carl Bereiter and Marlene Scardamalia, *The Psychology of Written Composition* (Hillsdale, NJ: Erlbaum, 1987).

5. MaryAnn Murphy, "Envisionment Building in Math: A Reflection on the Year," *The Partnership Community* 3, no. 1 (2010): 3, http://www.albany.edu/cela/publication/p4l_newletter_10_2010.pdf.

*Chapter Five*

# Purposeful Planning

*Designing a Coherent and Connected Curriculum*

> *At best a formal curriculum can provide an overview of experiences and topics for conversation.* [1]

The guiding principle underlying all of the classroom activities in this book is that only instruction that emphasizes higher-order thinking skills will prepare students for their future education, careers, and participation in civic society. Certainly the policy makers and educators in states that have adopted the Common Core Standards also believe that this is a priority. Local educators, however, often face increasing and sometimes conflicting demands as they try to achieve this worthy goal.

The Standards delineate the kinds of achievements required for students to be prepared to enter and succeed in college and the workforce, including the ability to learn on their own. But they neither mandate nor provide guidance on the thinking and planning that teachers need to do in order to support all students in their development as independent learners. So far this book has focused primarily on planning for shorter-term activities—those to use daily or across a unit. This chapter focuses on the longer-range planning needed in order to provide a coherent and cohesive curriculum across a semester, a year, or more.

Such planning involves not only teaching students to become disciplinary thinkers, as stressed in earlier chapters, but also designing a curriculum organized around the big ideas of a discipline. This chapter does not suggest specific classroom activities but rather guides you through thinking about your curriculum as a way to engage students in higher-order thinking appropriate to the discipline(s) you teach. Arthur Applebee, among others, calls this "apprenticing" students into each discipline and suggests that it is through this apprenticing that your students will get the most out of your curriculum.[2]

For some of you, this may require that you begin to think explicitly about yourself as a mathematician or health professional, a scientist or social scientist, a language specialist or musician—the practitioner of whatever field(s) of study you teach. Your specialty is still teaching, but you also look at information in a particular way because of what you have studied and chosen to specialize in. By articulating the way specialists in your field(s) read a text of any kind or share information, you can help your students understand how to do so in that subject.

Elementary- and intermediate-level teachers who teach multiple subjects can do this as well. You can introduce the idea that different disciplines approach research and writing in different ways and use language appropriate to that particular subject. For example, call a hands-on science activity an "experiment" and log the data as scientists do. Overt actions like these apprentice students into a subject, bringing them "inside" the discipline rather than studying it from the outside.[3]

Creating a classroom workshop for teaching disciplinary thinking begins with rethinking the curriculum. In order to engage students in thinking and writing about significant topics within any discipline, curriculum planning needs to focus on creating experiences that encourage significant conversations—"curriculum as conversation"—not a catalog of dates or facts but an ongoing examination of major ideas. Use these major concepts to inform and shape inquiry and provide anchors for learning. Doing this will develop higher-order thinking and make students rethink what they have learned previously, as well as generate new knowledge.[4]

Thus far this book has been encouraging you to work with your colleagues, and with good reason. One reason is that collaboration benefits *you*—not only by helping you solve instructional problems; collaborating about curriculum can reinvigorate your subject, enrich your own thinking, help you find ways to streamline, and reinforce your efforts in the classroom.

Even more important are the benefits to students, as teacher collaboration can shape curriculum and instruction in a more effective and engaging way. In fact, a collaborative school culture is one of the characteristics that marks the difference between higher- and average-performing schools. Students especially benefit when all teachers offer a coherent approach—particularly when instruction across all grades and subjects fosters a minds-on, every-student-always-thinking approach.[5]

## SUPPORTING STUDENTS AS DISCIPLINARY THINKERS

What does it mean to be a disciplinary thinker? How does a scientist, historian, mathematician, or writer think? How do social scientists read primary resources? How do scientists collect data? How do mathematicians demonstrate mathematical reasoning? And how does a teacher teach these skills in any content area?

With the Common Core Standards emphasizing content literacy and higher-level thinking, it is even more imperative that teachers strive to develop disciplinary thinkers. Partnership for Literacy coaches have always encouraged teachers to do this by first viewing themselves as writers, scientists, mathematicians, or social scientists and then teaching their specific ways of thinking, knowing, and doing to students. It is important to make this approach to content explicit for students.

It was during a professional development meeting focused on critical thinking that Karen realized that the ways of thinking in her discipline were different from those of colleagues outside of her department. As the discussion progressed, it became obvious that English language arts (ELA), science, mathematics, and social studies teachers did not approach gathering information, analyzing it, and drawing conclusions from it in the same way. Nor did they ask questions, solve problems, or present findings in the same way. Thus, Karen realized that she needed to be more explicit in teaching her students to be critical thinkers in social studies.

Karen looked for ways to apprentice her students as social scientists; using the academic language appropriate for social studies was an obvious first step. But she found that she also needed to shift the way she thought about her role and began looking for opportunities to support her students' development of the reasoning used by social scientists. The effect on students quickly became evident: they began making inferences, discussing information, answering questions, and refining their conclusions as apprentices in the social sciences. Karen's own passion for her subject was rekindled and that, in turn, sparked active engagement by her students.

When you think about what it might mean to apprentice your students into a subject, try thinking about it as teaching them to be *doers* of that discipline—be the mathematician or scientist or literary critic—instead of learning *about* that subject. Then you will be teaching them to think, talk, and write like specialists in the discipline. This means, in part, using the academic language appropriate to each discipline. For example, ask students to "provide evidence" to support a conclusion instead of just asking, "Why?"

Teaching in this way may be a fundamental change for you. For one thing, you must make the ways of thinking and knowing and discussing within your content area(s) overt and teach that to your students. This means moving away from "covering" content to providing opportunities for students to grapple with the most significant content as specialists in each subject area would. In this way, they really learn the content and acquire understanding and foundational knowledge that will last a lifetime, not just until the next summary test.

The relevant topics for discussion, what counts as appropriate evidence, and what kinds of arguments are effective will differ from one discipline to another. Thinking about the subject(s) you teach, ask yourself questions like,

- How do _____ present conclusions or findings?
- How do _____ record data?
- What resources do _____ use to gather data?
- What are some differences between one discipline and another—between your discipline and others—in terms of vocabulary, research methods, and what counts as evidence and how it is presented?
- How do people in your field determine the validity and reliability of a resource (e.g., a website)?
- What determines the validity of a conclusion?
- How do _____ know when they have enough evidence to draw a valid conclusion?
- How do _____ deal with new evidence, technologies, questions, and/or ways of thinking?

Helping students understand the ways of thinking and conversing within a content area puts knowledge in context and gives them the tools to integrate and use what they learn. Grappling with ideas the way a specialist would deepens students' understanding and requires them to use appropriate academic vocabulary and think critically. When you require students to go beyond building knowledge to doing something with that knowledge, they learn the content better and develop ways of thinking that will help them be successful in future schooling and careers.

It is impossible to promote these abilities without incorporating purposeful discussions in instruction. Discussions that focus on big-picture thinking and require increased student engagement change the student role from what students may have become used to. Students of every age, but especially those in the upper elementary and middle school years who are still exploring life's possibilities and their own potential, are energized by this approach and strive to achieve the higher standard required of aspiring historians, scientists, or mathematicians.

In building academic literacy by teaching disciplinary thinking, teachers must allow students opportunities to wrestle with resources, content, and questions in order to develop a conceptual understanding of a topic. In this way, students begin to make connections, build knowledge, and participate as practitioners of the discipline. An envisionment-building classroom, a classroom that engages students in higher-level thinking by promoting discussion using the stances described in Chapter 3, develops academic literacy.

## RETHINKING THE CURRICULUM

### Starting with the Big Ideas

As teachers help students become apprentices in a discipline, it becomes necessary to view the curriculum differently. To engage students in learning about significant topics, curriculum planning should focus on creating experiences that encourage significant conversations about the content. A helpful way to think about it is teaching with the big ideas in mind. Materials must also be connected to and integral to the big ideas. Building connections in day-to-day instruction supports student learning, but even more effective is doing that within an overall curriculum that is cohesive day to day, week to week, month to month, and year to year.

*Identifying the big-picture themes or questions in a course of study can be surprisingly difficult. One way to approach the task is to focus first on the ways of thinking within a discipline rather than focusing on specific content. One group of sixth-grade teachers asked Partnership for Literacy coaches to help them tackle the process of articulating some overarching ideas for the year's social studies content.*

*Primarily teachers of ELA, they were overwhelmed by the sheer extent of the social studies content and were unsure about what topics they should emphasize. They had identified the major units throughout the year, each of which dealt with a significant civilization. With Karen's guidance, they designed a way to structure gathering knowledge about a culture.*

*Gathering and classifying information by geographic, economic, political, and sociological features provides an important framework for examining the life of any people. In this case, the framework encouraged students to make connections between the categories. How does the geography of a place affect the economic life of its people? How did this change over time? What economic factors affected the government of a people and vice versa? How did daily life reflect the religious beliefs of the people?*

*The teachers decided to center instruction around the ways of thinking of an anthropologist. Developing a framework and making it overt for students provided a thoughtful path for moving through the year as they led their students in examining a variety of cultures as budding anthropologists.*

This group of teachers was well on the way to creating a curriculum that centered around big ideas. Student knowledge of social studies became larger than a collection of facts and focused on using research to develop and articulate understandings about the peoples they studied.

Another group of social studies teachers, which included Karen and her colleagues, worked collaboratively to organize their content around big ideas. One year this group organized five units that overlapped chronologically and required seventh-grade students to circle back and link each new topic to the current one. For the Grade 7 curriculum, which covered chronological history from Native Americans in North America to the Civil War, the big ideas were

- prove that Native Americans had cultures worthy of respect
- assess the impact of contact on Native Americans and Europeans
- evaluate diversity within the New England, Middle and Southern colonies
- explain the extent to which the new nation achieved democracy from 1800 to 1848
- evaluate Abraham Lincoln's attempts to preserve the democracy

These ideas provided the "end" goal for a series of units. They pulled students into thinking and discussion. Engaging them in this way motivated students to want to go back and do the work necessary to support their thinking. Students gathered information on a variety of topics within each unit, all of which were necessary for them to reflect on the bigger idea they were exploring. Each question or statement could be addressed in multiple ways and always led to more questions. As students addressed each topic, they themselves kept raising the even bigger idea of equal justice for all, which came to be the unifying theme for the year.

Another year the teachers chose one overarching idea: "together and apart in times of change." It, too, helped students approach the content as budding social scientists examining first European settlement and then the establishment and growth of the new nation, including its impact on native inhabitants.

Teachers could just as effectively have used "appreciating diversity" as the overarching theme. It is not that the big idea does not matter, but there are many from which to choose. The best advice is to be flexible and embrace the connections your students make; you may find new ideas emerging that you can capitalize on this year or in the future.

> In mathematics, Ron's big idea was to relate the major concepts students were learning to the world that students knew. For example, when working with percentages, he charged students with using percentages to explain the likely fate of the world's pandas in the wild, given the rate at which China's industrialization is reducing the natural habitat of pandas. Students' presentations to the class (and invited adults) had to demonstrate mathematical thinking. Assignments like this also offer the potential to collaborate with science, social studies, and/or ELA teachers. A similar exercise might do the same for polar bears or penguins, given the melting of polar ice.

Some teachers have been able to identify a single overarching theme that can cross many—or even all—subject areas. For example, for students in the tween and early teen years, an idea like "growth" is not only relevant, it can also provide coherence in each subject as well as across subjects, including health, character education, and career exploration.[6] The list below suggests some potential big questions or ideas relevant to many disciplines.

Examples of Potential Overarching Ideas

- Heroes, villains, and the nature of good and evil
- Making good choices
- Facing and overcoming adversity
- Is the world a village?

- How we shape the environment—how the environment shapes us
- How math relates to the real world
- Conflict
- Personal freedom versus social responsibility
- Self, family, community, nation—priorities and choices
- The pursuit of justice
- Who causes societal (or scientific) change—groups or individuals?
- Abstraction/patterns/structures
- Change/growth

The challenge for ELA teachers may be less one of finding an overarching idea to connect the various texts and genres studied in any year and more one of figuring out what it means to apprentice students into the study of ELA. The example in Chapter 1 of Johanna creating a classroom community of literate learners provides one example.

A second example comes from Kerri, an ELA teacher who, for 10 years, as part of her curriculum, has been apprenticing poets. Set up like a coffee house (complete with couches, tables, and refreshments) in the cafeteria, the Java Jive she hosts gives student poets an opportunity to present their best poems at an annual open mike in front of friends and family—just like in the real world.

## Thinking beyond the Textbook

A curriculum that apprentices students into a discipline and leads to higher-order thinking has to be rich in both quality and quantity of materials and experiences. While a textbook lays out the content to be "covered," it does not necessarily draw attention to the biggest ideas or concepts within the content area. Providing multiple resources always helps students to grapple with and better understand the content and allows you to differentiate instruction as your normal way of instructing. Prior chapters provided multiple suggestions for ways to engage your students as active participants in using these materials to learn.

## Quality of Materials

Earlier chapters asked you to consider the quality of the materials you have been using to see if there is enough meat on their bones for your students to have something to chew on. Ask yourself if the text, video, or other material intrigues you. If not, then it might not work for your students either. If the text is required, see if you can find something to pair it with (e.g., the way Karen paired *Encounter* with Columbus's journal) so that the two can rub against each other and give students a different perspective or some sort of contrast.

Materials of different genres offer such contrasts. Returning to Emma Lazarus's "The New Colossus" as an example, depending on your primary discipline and the age of your students, you might consider using it with a textbook or first-person account of immigration, a map related to immigration, and/or a statistical table. A children's picture book such as *If the World Were a Village* provides math students a wealth of examples to turn into statistical data, for example, of world population growth over millennia or centuries.

For students learning English or with limited experience of a new topic or concept, consider using short videos or photos—something as simple as showing what a Midwestern factory farm looks like before studying food production in the United States. (Depending on where you teach and where your students are from, they may have very different images of "farm" than what spreads over much of the central United States.) And don't rule out unconventional sources like YouTube or TeacherTube videos; just be sure you know how the material will advance the learning of the content and the experience of learning it.

## Quantity of Material

As for quantity, U.S. curricula are famously said to be a mile wide and an inch deep. Given that situation, the issue of quantity is probably the hardest to grapple with and the one you can least afford to tackle alone. Using the ideas in this book and along with your colleagues, consider the most important concepts in the curriculum for your grade and subject. Then work to find big ideas that will allow you to cover more ground by addressing topics through minds-on activities that truly engage every student in wrestling with big questions.

In this process, students need to learn the factual material. This does not mean that you do not directly teach content. Rather, effective instruction mixes direct instruction, practice application, and authentic tasks as needed.[7]

Quantity also refers to figuring out how much material you need in order to sustain the curricular conversation about an important topic for students at your grade level(s). Sometimes excerpts are enough. From Columbus's journal, for example, Karen used only the excerpt provided by the textbook; she then supplemented that with cartoons and other primary sources based on the questions her students were raising during discussions.

Dan, using only a photo of a Union soldier, got across more of the information about the experiences and background of Civil War soldiers than many pages of text may have done.[8] Pat needed to read aloud only a short section of Bill Bryson's "The Cell" to capture her intermediate-level students' interest and desire to learn more. You will find that you can focus and trim by constantly asking yourself, "What do I really want my students to learn, and how can I best organize the materials so that maximum learning can happen?"

## Reflection and Action

Thinking about your curriculum, to what extent do the materials you have been using

- provide a sense of direction from what has been studied before to what will come next
- relate to important discussions in the field as a whole
- relate to students' lives and the larger school/local community
- support students to consider material from various cognitive stances (see Chapter 3)
- ask students to make clear and accurate contributions to the on-going discussion—contributions that they can support by relevant argument and evidence
- cover topics or concepts that will sustain meaningful discussion
- provide a variety of materials
- offer an appropriate breadth and depth of material in order to sustain discussion

## COLLABORATION

In schools where collaboration is expected and where colleagues are given opportunities to work and meet together, students perform better. Collaboration is an opportunity for teachers to have meaningful conversations about teaching, and many studies have found it to be critical for ensuring student success. Based on the authors' experiences, as well as the research of others, this book often refers teachers to the importance of collaborating. Teachers work better when working together with other teachers, thinking reflectively about curriculum and students and how to meet their needs in mastering their learning.[9]

Collaborating with your colleagues will likely look different in every setting, and no book can anticipate your particular situation, including the level of structural support for collaboration. But it can offer an example or two and hope that from them you get inspiration and ideas for what you might do in your school. Our first example comes from a middle school team. With Eija (their Partnership for Literacy coach), they have written about their experience; therefore, the vignette below provides only a brief summary.[10]

*After two years of working together to provide the kind of instruction advocated in this book, Laurie, Dave, Monica, and Randy saw a need to do more. Their team of 100 students was accustomed to rich, envisionment-building discussions in each of their core classes, but the teaching team wanted to up the ante in order to better prepare them for the rigors of high school—and beyond.*

*Working with Eija, they first asked themselves individually, "What do I want my students to know at the end of the year?" and "How am I going to teach that?" After discussing their responses with each other, they decided that their major focus would be critical thinking in several dimensions—in discussion, in writing, in each discipline, and in students' awareness of their own thinking. At the beginning of the year, they began by asking the students in each of their classes, "What does it mean to be a critical thinker in science?" "In math?" "In social studies?" "In English?"*

*Concerned that they needed to extend critical thinking to writing and to make clear to students both the similarities and differences across disciplines, together they developed ways to teach and assess that skill. They devised a rubric that they could use across their disciplines while modifying it for each subject. They devised a three-level system—(1) knowledge, comprehension, application; (2) analysis; (3) synthesis and evaluation—that they shared with their students, providing action verbs indicative of each level and examples of writing that demonstrated the skills at each level.*

*At the end of the year, they asked their students to reflect on the year and its focus on critical thinking and probed how students' ideas of what it means to be a critical thinker had changed. They concluded that because of their "common vocabulary, expectations, and ways to give feedback, students are doing more higher-level thinking and are more aware of their own learning."*[11] *Student comments, as reported by the team, spoke of the importance of discussion in giving them more ideas to write about and in their coming to understand that they could always do more, think more.*

If you are already working in a collaborative setting, perhaps you have been sharing this book with colleagues and, hopefully, trying things together, brainstorming, and troubleshooting. If that is not your situation, here are some ideas for how you might start a conversation and begin to bring some coherence to the instructional program for your students.

## Propose an Integrated Lesson or Unit

Approach a colleague or colleagues who teach the same students as you and see if there is a topic that logically can be addressed from your different perspectives. Suggest coordinating in some way so that the students (a) see the connection(s) and (b) come to understand the different ways to approach the topic and think about it in each discipline. You will need to make this explicit to your students, as they will not just intuit it. And at first you may need to explain it for the other discipline(s) as well.

Examples of topics relevant to multiple disciplines that come to mind are motion (physical education, science, ELA, music, art), structures (biology, health, social studies, math, music, art), any topic related to difficult choices (social sciences, health, ELA, math). Or it could be something as topic specific as Ron's panda and percentages lesson. Start wherever you find a logical opportunity.

## Work with Your Department and/or Grade-Level Team

Whether your district, school, or department has mapped your curriculum or not, commencing or returning to that work with colleagues is a good place to start or continue collaborating within your grade level(s) and/or discipline(s). Fine tuning curriculum is never done. Standards change, student needs change, important issues within a discipline change.

(Even our understanding of ancient history is still changing because of new archaeological discoveries. Think about the teaching opportunities—in science, social studies, math, health—created by the discovery of the ice man on the Austrian-Italian border in 1991 or, in science, the completion of mapping of the human genome.)

Local or state assessments might show gaps in skills or knowledge that can be addressed by realigning the curriculum. The Common Core Standards can provide guidance to you and your colleagues as you seek curriculum congruence and alignment.

## Open Your Door and Invite Colleagues In

Another way to begin or enhance a dialogue with colleagues is to open your classroom doors and invite them in to see a minds-on classroom in action. Instructional leaders, especially, benefit from seeing what a truly engaged learning community of youngsters looks and sounds like.

## Plan a Learning Celebration

One nonthreatening way to find out what your colleagues think is important and how they teach is to have an end-of-the-year celebration of learning. This is something that you may want to propose to your principal or curriculum coordinator. In such a celebration, all teachers are invited to showcase learning in their classrooms.

A Gallery Walk works well for this, especially because it provides opportunities for those visiting each display to post a comment. This can be done using sticky notes or a separate piece of paper so as not to deface the teacher's work. Even better would be an electronic forum (discussion board, blog, Facebook page) to encourage dialogue at the time, as well as in the future, perhaps to begin the next school year. Each teacher prepares a display—for example, a poster board, although a video or other electronic display is also suitable—using classroom examples to demonstrate areas of student thinking and growth across the year.

Not only does such a celebration show appreciation for the hard (and too often unrecognized) work that teachers do, it also provides a way for teachers to see what their colleagues are doing. In a faculty that is not used to working together—and has few opportunities to do so—it may open some connections. (And, of course, even if you are working together and share instructional approaches, it is still a good idea for celebrating and solidifying, as well as learning from each other.)

## SUMMARY

This chapter stresses the importance of apprenticing students as disciplinary thinkers. Doing so requires thinking about the curriculum as focused on the big ideas and common threads within any discipline. Teachers who collaborate with colleagues are better able to provide such a curriculum and the kinds of experiences that support students to be social scientists, scientists, or mathematicians. Teaching to the big ideas and offering opportunities to think and work across disciplines develops higher-order thinking skills for students.

## NOTES

1. Arthur N. Applebee, *Curriculum as Conversation: Transforming Traditions of Teaching and Learning* (Chicago: University of Chicago Press, 1996), 83.

2. Ibid. Also see Barbara Rogoff, *Apprenticeship in Thinking: Cognitive Development in Social Context* (New York: Oxford University Press, 1990).

3. Cynthia Shanahan and Timothy Shanahan, "Does Disciplinary Literacy Have a Place in Elementary School?" *Reading Teacher* 67, no. 8 (2014): 636–39, doi:10.1002/trtr.1257. Timothy Shanahan and Cynthia Shanahan, "Teaching Disciplinary Literacy to Adolescents: Rethinking Content-Area Literacy," *Harvard Educational Review* 78, no. 1 (Spring 2008): 40–59.

4. Applebee, *Curriculum as Conversation*; Fenwick English, *Deciding What to Teach and Test: Developing, Aligning, and Leading the Curriculum, 3rd ed.* (Thousand Oaks, CA: Corwin, 2010).

5. Judith A. Langer, *Getting to Excellent: How to Create Better Schools* (New York: Teachers College Press, 2004); Kristen C. Wilcox, *What Works in Middle School Science: Preparing Students to Become the Next Generation of Scientists* (Albany: State University of New York, 2009), http://www.albany.edu/nykids/files/MiddleSchool_Science_FullReport.pdf.

6. For example, see Elizabeth Close, Molly Hull, and Judith A. Langer, "Writing and Reading Relationships in Literacy Learning: Theory and Research in Practice," In *Learning to Write, Writing to Learn*, ed. Roselmina Indrisano and Jeanne R. Paratore (Newark, DE: International Reading Association, 2005), in which an ELA teacher (Hull) explains how she shaped instruction for the year to relate to the idea of change. Both her Partnership for Literacy coach (Close) and the Partnership for Literacy founder and researcher (Langer) comment on Hull's narrative, giving readers additional insight into the whys and wherefores of Hull's approach.

7. Judith A. Langer et al., *Guidelines for Teaching Middle and High School Students to Read and Write Well* (Albany: Center on English Learning & Achievement, 2000), http://www.albany.edu/cela/publication/brochure/guidelines.pdf.

8. Dan King, "Drummer Boys: Creating Historical Fiction and Studying Historical Documents," *Middle Level Learning*, May/June 2010: 10–12.

9. Kristen C. Wilcox and Janet I. Angelis, *Best Practices from High-Performing Middle Schools: How Successful Schools Remove Obstacles and Create Pathways to Learning* (New York: Teachers College Press, 2009); Janet I. Angelis and Kristen C. Wilcox, "Poverty, Performance, and Frog Ponds: What Best Practice Research Tells Us about Their Connections," *Kappan* 13, no. 3 (2011): 26–31.

10. David Ackley et al., "Literacy across the Curriculum: A Team Approach to Promoting Critical Thinking," *Educator's Voice* 3 (Spring 2010): 2–9.

11. Ibid., 9.

*Chapter Six*

# Purposeful Leadership

*Supporting Effective Instructional Practices*

> *A leader who comes and sits next to you and says, "How can I help you?" is a leader.*[1]

Although designed primarily to be a coach-in-a-pocket for teachers, this book also can serve anyone with responsibilities for instruction, including instructional leaders, whose roles are key to building a school's capacity for promoting higher-order thinking. The preceding chapters spoke mainly to teachers; this chapter addresses instructional leaders. It suggests to those leaders not only some of the structural features they can put in place to support teachers working to implement the approaches advocated in Chapters 1–5 but also ways to build individual competencies during and after classroom observations.

As suggested by the book's title, the overall goal is to provide teachers with instructional strategies that promote academic literacy and higher-order thinking skills. Key to the success of all of those strategies is connecting reading, writing, listening, thinking, and speaking so that every student is not only engaged with the content but mindfully processing that content in ways appropriate to the subject at hand. In a nutshell, this means that in each subject, teachers should be "apprenticing" students in that subject—*being* the mathematician rather than doing math.

Thinking about teaching and learning in this way often means changing the way curriculum and instruction are organized and thought about by teachers, students, and administrators. A major goal of this chapter is to advise instructional leaders about what to look for as they observe teachers and students in classrooms, as well as suggestions for productive follow-up. Some of the suggestions are things to look for while moving through the building or conducting a walk-through or short observation; others are related to observations that might be part of your formal performance review process.

To use the suggestions in this chapter, instructional leaders must be familiar with the book's overall approach and its underpinnings. It relies on the material you have gleaned from Chapters 1–5.

As a building leader, you are in a unique position to be familiar with students and classrooms across grade levels and subjects, able to discern growth over time or to see strengths in different subject areas. You also likely are keenly aware of the students about whose academic learning and growth you and others are most concerned. Consider these students, especially, as you observe students whose teachers are trying the strategies suggested in this book.

The remainder of this chapter is organized according to the topics introduced in the earlier chapters. Each section provides a brief overview, which is neither intended nor able to replace the material covered in the earlier chapter.

## STUDENT VOICE (CHAPTER 1)

Chapter 1 advises teachers to start by ensuring that every student in their class(es) feels safe to voice his or her thoughts. In order for students to really engage with academic work, they must feel safe enough to take the risks necessary in order to engage in thinking with each other. Part of your role as an instructional leader is to ensure that teachers feel safe enough to support students to feel safe to engage in this way.

Teachers who are working to bring student voice to the forefront of their classrooms can use a variety of activities and tools to foster a classroom learning community. When you are observing their classrooms, here are some things to look for:

- How is the classroom arranged? Can students make eye contact with each other?
- Are they able to work in pairs or small groups (i.e., they are not in rows facing only the teacher)?
- Is a list of ground rules for how to take part in a discussion posted for all to see?
- Are students using conversation vocabulary such as, "I agree with what you said because . . . ?"

When the teacher is using paired or small group work, are students talking with each other about the ideas or questions posed by the teacher? Has she or he scaffolded the activity so that students know what to do and all of the students can engage? Take special note of any students about whose progress you are most concerned—not just those with challenges, such as English learners and special education students, but also those who need more challenge. Watch the pairs and small groups. Are they productive for all of the participants?

If you have conducted an informal walk-through, you have, of course, seen only a snapshot of what is happening in any classroom. If the answers to the questions above are affirmative, you might want to simply send a note to the teacher highlighting what you saw, but if you did not observe these activities, you might initiate a conversation to give the teacher an opportunity to explain the thinking and planning that went into the lesson you observed.

In the latter case, some things to ask about include whether students have had a hand in developing classroom procedures, including ground rules for discussion; whether students are encouraged and given opportunities to reflect on classroom processes and how those processes help them learn; whether students and teacher ever debrief an activity together to discuss its pros and cons in supporting student thinking.

When a teacher is just beginning to use the approaches advocated in this book, such conversations can focus on how involved students are in their own learning. Your observations can help support teachers to reflect on this, identifying strengths and targeting next steps to try tomorrow and in the next days in order to make instruction more effective. Perhaps more important, you can open up conversations about teachers' overall learning goals and how a particular lesson is helping all of the students meet those expectations.

As you observe individual teachers' classrooms over time, you will find that you are able to provide feedback on progress and/or facilitate discussions that will encourage them to open their classrooms more to student voices.

Hopefully, teachers who are adopting the approach advocated in this book are setting goals that are aligned with promoting academic literacy and higher-order thinking. The foundation rests on every student being minds on and expected to fully participate in a classroom characterized by purposeful student talk. Formal evaluation of teachers should include their own reflections as well as student artifacts (e.g., Journal Jots, Tickets Out, videoed discussions) that reflect student engagement in their own learning.

## ENGAGING ACTIVITIES (CHAPTER 2)

Chapter 2 suggests several activities to engage all learners, with the caution that each activity needs to serve an instructional purpose beyond just being fun or engaging for students. So, for example, if a teacher is using Think-Pair-Share:

- Is he or she giving students time to first think and capture their thinking in writing before sharing?
- Is the material engaging or complex?
- Does it require thoughtfulness?
- Is the purpose of a Think-Pair-Share activity apparent to you and the students?

In general, has the teacher helped students understand the purposes of instructional activities so that they have internalized them and transitions from one to another are accomplished efficiently? For example, when prompted to do so, do students quickly move into pairs or small groups? Has this become a natural part of the classroom flow?

Chapter 2 also offers tools and activities to help students read and understand informational and complex texts, a requirement of the Common Core Standards.

- Has the teacher provided the scaffolding to enable all of the students to engage with these texts?
- For example, has she or he asked a purpose question so that the students know what they are reading for?
- Do they have scaffolds to help them gather information from the text—whether print narrative, video, chart, or image?

As you observe classrooms over time:

- Do you see students using these scaffolds on their own or using them purposefully in other classrooms or situations?
- Are students being encouraged and supported to ask questions about the material they are engaging with or are all questions teacher generated?

In a short walk-through or brief observation you may not have opportunity to observe everything listed above. However, if you consider questions like these when debriefing with a teacher or conducting a more formal evaluation, together you can work to construct a classroom that is learner centered and meets the needs of different learners requiring varying levels of support and/or challenge.

In terms of documentary evidence related to teachers' goals, artifacts might include student Quick Writes, Written Conversations, papers showing student use of reader's marks/video viewing guides, lesson plans using paired texts, and the like.

## DISCUSSION (CHAPTER 3)

Chapter 3 introduces a framework for facilitating discussions that promote academic learning and higher-order thinking. It includes five cognitive stances that readers take on as they engage with a text: stepping in, exploring, stepping back and rethinking what they know, stepping back and objectifying the experience, and going beyond.

And it provides a scaffold for teachers to use to plan and conduct such discussions called an envisionment-building guide (EBG). Using this scaffold/framework, a teacher can facilitate a discussion that moves students from simply recalling factual material to analyzing, synthesizing, evaluating, and generally processing the material in ways appropriate to the content area.

Planning and leading such a discussion takes practice, and instructional and other building leaders can provide opportunities for practice outside of the classroom. There are several ways to do this. For example, you might read this book or any of its chapters with an entire faculty, department, or grade level and have an envisionment-building discussion, with any member(s) of the group taking responsibility for drafting the EBG.

Or you might draft an EBG in order to facilitate a faculty meeting discussion about a particular pressing issue (e.g., the increasing number of students living in poverty or an influx of English learning students). Such modeling by an administrator or building leader not only provides a rich discussion experience for teachers but also signals support for conducting such discussions with students, especially if the modeling is made explicit.

Teachers who are trying envisionment-building discussions need time to develop their skills and, maybe just as important, they benefit from collaborating with peers. Building leaders can support this by freeing a second teacher to cofacilitate a discussion with a colleague. Both teachers and coaches benefit from the opportunity to plan, conduct, and debrief the discussion. Or a volunteer or volunteers might share a videotaped snippet of a classroom discussion as part of a faculty or professional development meeting. You can remind teachers to employ the strategies they are using in the classroom in order to facilitate their own professional growth.

Additionally, if you have only a small group of teachers trying these methods, once they achieve a recognizable change in student engagement and thinking, you may want to involve more teachers. One way to accomplish this is to have some key volunteers share their work with others—the whole faculty or a smaller group such as a grade-level team or department. They might even become mentors to colleagues beginning the process. Distributing leadership and developing the capacity of teacher-leaders is an essential responsibility of principals, in particular.

Also, showcasing student achievements at a Parent Teacher Association (PTA) meeting or at a school board meeting could spark some interest among the community for broader adoption of this research-based approach to fostering learning and higher-order thinking.

When you visit a classroom in which the teacher is facilitating an envisionment-building discussion, look first at the classroom set-up and student participation (Chapters 1 and 2). Try mapping the interactions taking place. Does the map look like a web with lines going from multiple participants, or does it look like the spokes of a wheel, with one person (usually the teacher) as the axel?

Other things to look for:

- Does it seem that students are prepared for the discussion?
- Are they asking and responding to meaningful questions?
- Is the teacher allowing time for students to ask their questions before jumping in?
- Do you see an EBG in the teacher's hand?
- What is he or she doing to raise the bar or up the ante on student thinking?
- Following the discussion, does the teacher allow time for reflection about the discussion itself, the process, and the learning?

If a teacher is early in the process of trying envisionment-building discussions, remember that good discussion facilitation happens over time and with practice, debriefing, and refining. What you should see over time is increased ownership by students of the questions and the learning, not the I-R-E (teacher *initiates* question—student *responds*—teacher *evaluates*) "discussions" typical in most classrooms.[2]

As a teacher and students become more adept at envisionment-building discussions, look for higher-level questions from students, spontaneous use of discipline-appropriate vocabulary, and students being more reflective about process and content as they delve deeper into the subject matter. The teacher will still be an integral part of the discussion, but her or his role will shift to providing encouragement to students, ensuring that all of the cognitive stances are addressed and that every student is able to participate.

In debriefing with teachers, areas to discuss include activities that preceded the discussion, including what materials the teacher had provided to motivate students intellectually and to enable all students to participate (differentiation). Another important area to explore is where the teacher had planned for the discussion to lead and how that might have changed given the discussion itself. An effective envisionment-building discussion should push students to further explore the concepts and themes involved in the particular subject.

As suggested above, it takes time to become adept at facilitating envisionment-building discussions, so careful observation and feedback that notes areas of strength are important in order to encourage continued development. You play a key role in encouraging teachers to persevere. Take the time to have conversations with individuals and groups of teachers about their experiences. Give them opportunities to reflect on their own and students' growth and to help you better understand this dynamic and complex process.

Documents that teachers might provide in order to show evidence of progress toward their goals could include EBGs and related graphic organizers (e.g., T-charts), as well as videotaped classroom discussions.

## ASSIGNMENTS (CHAPTER 4)

Chapter 4 builds on the earlier chapters by reminding teachers that every tool, activity, and assignment should relate to the larger themes of their curriculum, pushing them to keep in mind the bigger questions as they plan their day-to-day instruction. It also reemphasizes the importance of asking students to use writing to develop, refine, and capture their thinking so that they can share their thoughts with others and/or refer to them at a later time.

Offering such instruction requires a variety of resources so that all students can access the curriculum (e.g., texts of varying degrees of difficulty and different genres on the same topic, graphic displays, audio and video resources).

- Do you observe students purposefully using these resources?
- What do you see on the classroom bulletin boards and walls? Is there evidence of student work and thinking—for example, posters, diagrams, chart paper reflecting previous discussion or thinking?
- Do students have learning logs or journals or notes that they can refer to?

In reflecting with a teacher, have you observed or discovered that she or he has provided opportunities for students to take stock of their learning? This does not mean a summative or even formative test but a meaningful activity that allows students to draw some conclusions about the content they have been studying (e.g., a unit of study).

Activities such as those suggested in the latter half of Chapter 4 help students consolidate what they have learned, articulate their thinking, and share it with others in ways appropriate to a particular discipline. These activities include Gallery Walk, Carousel, Stand and Deliver, and extended writing.

## FOSTERING COHERENCE (CHAPTER 5)

Chapter 5 speaks to teachers about the importance of three things: apprenticing students into the various disciplines, rethinking their curriculum as an extended conversation in the field, and the benefits of collaboration. As discussed in the introduction to this chapter, apprenticing students into the disciplines means teaching them to *be* scientists or mathematicians, and so on, rather than doing science or math. The remainder of this chapter focuses on two keys to building the coherence associated with higher student performance: coherence within the curriculum and coherence across grades and subjects.

## Rethinking the Curriculum to Be More Coherent

The curriculum is a work plan that is constantly in flux. Whether it needs to be altered to meet changing standards or to keep up with new research, the curriculum must be a living document.[3] And teachers need to be part of discussions that lead to curriculum changes.[4] Thus, administrators need to provide time for teachers to participate in such discussions, whether in professional development days, regularly scheduled meetings, or summer work.

As teachers use the approaches recommended in this book to apprentice students into a discipline, it becomes necessary to reexamine the curriculum in order to see how it can address the big questions or topics in a field. Chapter 5 recommends that teachers begin to think of their curriculum as a year-long conversation about the big ideas to be addressed within the content for the year. This means more than writing an "essential question" on the board each day.

When debriefing or reflecting with a teacher about where a particular activity or discussion came from, also include an exploration of where it is heading; in this way, you can reinforce for the teacher the need not only to identify the big ideas but to always teach with those big ideas in mind. The student work you are looking for in the classroom and as part of teachers' performance portfolios should also show that students are wrestling with the big ideas or concepts in the field and that they are processing information rather than just collecting facts.

## Collaboration across Grades and Subjects

When opportunities for collaboration are provided, teachers are more effective in incorporating new strategies into instruction. Individual teachers make a difference in student learning, but teachers working together have real impact on student achievement.[5] In a crowded school day, collaboration may not happen on its own.

Curriculum leaders, principals, department chairs, and staff developers, along with teachers themselves, must provide the vision, tools, and opportunity for meaningful collaboration to occur. Additionally, leaders need to periodically visit, if not participate within, the collaborative groups.

*In a job interview for a teaching position, Johanna was asked the following question by an administrator: "Who is one person who most influenced you as a teacher?" Reflecting on that experience, Johanna wrote:*

> As I thought about this question, I recalled the many teachers who had helped me become the teacher I wanted to be. I settled upon talking about a special education teacher who had helped me think about my lessons more thoughtfully so that I might better adapt them for the learning styles of different students, keeping in mind what I wanted them to come away with but also focusing upon their needs as learners—how to bring the material to them so they would find it stimulating, not frustrating; interesting, not deadly; meaningful, not meaningless—considering their needs, not mine.
>
> She and I met during our free periods or after school. Our dialogue was a give and take of ideas and "noticings" and together figuring out how to engage all students in learning from the very start and throughout an entire lesson. We thought together about materials we might employ and how to break down lessons into doable parts so that all students could benefit.
>
> By coming into my classroom, she helped me see what she saw and then thought with me about ways to help classified students be more successful in their work. It was a huge shift for me. I found myself becoming more effective in getting students to see how to create and shape their own learning. She helped me by modeling how she created learning aids to support students as they negotiated the different requirements of each course her students took.
>
> She also helped me look at the growth of the students and then to appreciate and understand the various challenges these

*students faced; she assisted me in thinking about how to help them meet those challenges with more confidence and ease. For my part, I was able to help her understand the curriculum and time frame I was working with, as well as the reason for the skills and practices I expected students to internalize and use and think with as a necessary means of making sense of the world.*

*At the orientation meeting for teachers new to the district, the same administrator explained he had asked that very question of all of us. And every single teacher he had hired had shared in some way how a colleague had made a difference in helping that teacher become the teacher she or he wanted to be.*

The administrator in this vignette demonstrated that in this district, it was expected that teachers were learners and that they all had something to share and to learn. He was key in hiring people who knew that, who wanted to work with their colleagues in unraveling ways to help students be more successful.

Although collaboration can be mandated, it is most productive when an administrator (most often it is the principal) provides the instructional leadership to promote it among faculty members. As much as teachers work to build a classroom learning community, principals and other building leaders should be working to build a professional learning community within their schools in which teachers can collaborate and learn how to become more effective.

## Establishing an Environment of Trust

The foundation of any community is trust. Trying new approaches can be risky for teachers, especially in today's environment of high-stakes testing. One way to promote trust is through a shared goal, a higher purpose. Principals, together with teachers, can establish that the focus of instruction will be to promote higher-order thinking. Encouraging teachers to try new instructional strategies in order to attain this goal puts the focus on the shared goal and helps to avoid a nonproductive focus on personal feelings or shortcomings.

Administrators can build trust by taking risks themselves in trying new approaches. For example, principals and other instructional leaders can try using the EBG discussion framework in faculty or department meetings. In doing so, they not only make themselves vulnerable, which helps establish reciprocal trust,[6] but gathering feedback from using the framework in such forums can provide valuable insights for teachers trying this new strategy in their classrooms.

*Providing the Logistics*

Teachers also benefit from visiting each other's classrooms to observe and provide feedback. Ensuring that there is coverage so that teachers can leave their classrooms to observe a colleague's sends the message that the work being done is essential for developing curriculum and practices that will benefit students.

Time before or after school can provide opportunities for teachers to plan and reflect together, and many teachers will voluntarily use these times, as most value the benefits of working together. Principals can signal support of collaboration by offering additional times for teachers to meet. Dedicating one faculty meeting a month for groups of collaborating teachers to meet and focus on their work is one way in which some school administrators have found the time.

*Recruiting Outside Knowledge*

Principals and other administrators also play a key role in providing professional development that is relevant to a school's overall goals and needs. In order to make effective changes in instructional practice, support must be provided in the form of expertise and/or materials. Some leaders provide texts for teachers to read and discuss in a study group and then incorporate new strategies in their classrooms, meeting again to debrief and support each other.

Others bring in outside speakers or workshop leaders. Although one-shot presentations have not proven effective in changing instruction, opportunities to interact with experts should not be overlooked. The ways instructional leaders build on those opportunities can then extend and develop new ideas.

Although this book was written to be a coach-in-a-pocket, it does not pretend to replace or equal the effectiveness of sustained, embedded coaching for teachers. Such coaches can come from within a school or district or from outside agencies or companies. Given that a coherent approach and program have a greater impact on student achievement than individual teachers alone can,[7] the most effective approach is an environment in which coaching for all is the norm.

## Reflection and Acknowledgment

Students need to reflect on how they think and what they have learned, and so do teachers. Principals and other instructional leaders can play an important role in prompting teachers to reflect on the new practices they are incorporating into instruction. Just as class discussions need to include student questions and thinking, teacher meetings need to include teacher questions and thinking. This will build overall capacity for improvement and enhance and stimulate participation in achieving the shared goal of the learning community.

Leaders who participate in teacher collaborative groups as they meet and work send the message that their work is valued and important. By meeting with teachers as they question and grow, a leader is more aware of the issues that teachers are facing and can then be more effective in supporting teachers in their professional growth.

Making public the use of new strategies and positive outcomes helps to encourage participation. Attending special events to showcase the achievements of students as a result of new practices is also important. Acknowledging efforts to improve practice encourages teachers to continue thinking and learning.

## SUMMARY

The best advice for instructional leaders is to understand what this book and its adopters are trying to accomplish, then support those efforts with existing structures and by creating new ones that will provide even greater support. Expect and reward incremental progress; start small, recognize small successes, and keep explicitly building toward more purposeful pedagogy in each and every classroom.

## NOTES

1. 99U, "Simon Sinek: Why Leaders Eat Last," YouTube presentation, December 4, 2013, https://www.youtube.com/watch?v=ReRcHdeUG9Y.

2. Mary Adler and Eija Rougle, *Building Literacy through Classroom Discussion: Research-Based Strategies for Developing Critical Readers and Thoughtful Writers in Middle School* (New York: Scholastic, 2005).

3. Fenwick English, *Deciding What to Teach and Test: Developing, Aligning, and Leading the Curriculum, 3rd ed.* (Thousand Oaks, CA: Corwin, 2010).

4. Anthony Bryk and Barbara Schneider, *Trust in Schools: A Core Resource for Improvement* (New York: Russell Sage Foundation, 2002).

5. Judith A. Langer, *Getting to Excellent: How to Create Better Schools* (New York: Teachers College Press, 2004).

6. Kristen C. Wilcox et al., *Comparing and Contrasting Odds-Beating Schools: Toward a Theory of Action* (Albany: State University of New York, 2015), http://www.albany.edu/nykids/files/brief.TOA.NYKids.pdf.

7. See note 5.

# Conclusion

This book was designed to be a coach-in-a-pocket for educators seeking to build strong academic literacy and higher-order thinking. Hopefully it has served you in this way, especially when you were looking for an approach to reengage a reluctant learner or a class of them. Please return to these pages again and again for a reminder of an idea that works; introduce it again and get all of your students thinking about important content and developing strong academic literacy skills all of the time. They will thank you for it.

Perhaps you have come to this point after having backtracked several times to rethink, retry, or renew an instructional tool. Perhaps you have internalized the suggestions and are already weaving them into your everyday practice or your ongoing work with teachers. The intent throughout the book was to suggest ways for individuals, as well as groups of teachers, to further develop their instructional competencies and, together, to increase a school's capacity for improved teaching and learning.

Like the team that tackled critical thinking, described in Chapter 5, teachers in the Partnership for Literacy generally need a year or two of using more minds-on instructional tools before they are ready to rethink the trajectory of their curriculum and how to make it more coherent. Once they do, however, they find renewed interest and purpose in their teaching, they recapture the joy, and become reenergized.

And the work becomes better balanced, because students do more of the thinking work and take more responsibility for their own learning and the learning atmosphere in the classroom. With practice, these new ways of thinking and doing teaching become a set of "new bones"; they become the way of being a teacher, and there is no turning back, no matter how the policies around you change.

# Appendix A

*Sample Lessons*

Chapter 3 provided an extended example of envisionment-building activities and tools drawn from Karen's middle-level social studies classroom. This appendix serves as a supplement to that chapter. It includes descriptions, envisionment-building guides (EBGs), and T-charts for science (biology), mathematics, and English language arts (ELA).

## AN ENVISIONMENT-BUILDING LESSON FOR SCIENCE

The focus for this unit of study is adaptation. It assumes that each student has previously researched the characteristics and habits of a particular bird and mammal living in their area. Before asking them to identify each bird's or mammal's adaptations to the habitat and climate of your area, capture their interest with a story. For example, you might use the picture book *Stellaluna* in which a fruit bat orphan named Stellaluna is raised in a nest with baby birds. Before discussing the story, have students complete the top section of the T-chart in Table A.1.

Then it's time to turn to nonfiction materials—for example, their textbook, a video, an article, and/or other texts—that deal with the topic of adaptation scientifically. Together these materials (fiction and nonfiction) promote critical thinking because the story offers a different—and nonscientific—perspective. Have students complete the second row of the T-chart, then continue the discussion using the EBG provided.

Conclude the discussion by having students answer the questions in the bottom row of the T-chart. Now students should have a good grasp of the concept of adaptation and should be able to apply that understanding in order to explain the adaptations of the birds and mammals they are studying.

| Before Discussion | After Discussion |
| --- | --- |
| What are your first impressions after hearing *Stellaluna?*[a] What questions do you have that we might discuss? | What do you think about adaptation now? <br><br> Who or what influenced your thinking? |
| **After Reading the Additional Texts** ||
| What are the words or phrases that signal adaptation? What questions do they raise? ||
| What are the themes that connect the texts? <br><br> What additional resources could add to this discussion? ||

[a] Or other fictional work that can capture student interest and provoke critical analysis.

**Table A.1. T-Chart to Support Student Understanding of Animal Adaptation**

## EBG for *Stellaluna* and Nonfiction Texts

*Stepping into a Text*

- Review the notes you recorded on the T-chart. What are your first impressions after hearing *Stellaluna*?
- What questions come to mind after hearing the text?

*Exploring a Text*

- How did Stellaluna adjust to her situation after the owl attack?
- How did Mama Bird react to Stellaluna?
- How are the fruit bat's adaptations different from the birds' adaptations? How are they the same?
- What was meant when the bat said, "Wrong for a bird, maybe, but not for a bat?"

*Stepping Back and Rethinking What You Know*

- How does the story illustrate the concept of adaptation? Of survival?
- How did the nonfiction text(s) expand your understanding of adaptation?
- What are the themes that connect the texts?

*Stepping Back and Objectifying the Experience*

- What words or illustrations seem more provocative to you?
- How scientifically accurate is the story?
- Which of the texts is more reliable? Why?
- How would a scientist react to the story of Stellaluna?

## Going Beyond

- If a mammal altered its behavior or diet in order to survive in its environment, would that transfer to other mammals of the species or to its offspring?
- Can changes made by individuals alter a species?
- What implications of adaptation or survival must we as scientists consider today?

## AN ENVISIONMENT-BUILDING LESSON FOR MATHEMATICS

The following activity, variations of which are often used in math classes and which addresses at least two of the mathematics standards, lends itself especially well to a student-centered discussion in mathematics. This approach is key to helping students understand adding and subtracting positive and negative integers at a level beyond simply memorizing the rules for manipulating them.

Divide students into groups of two or three and give each group a handful of white beans and a handful of red beans. Give the following directions:

White beans = positive integers
Red beans = negative integers

Ask students to solve a series of straightforward problems that deal with the addition and subtraction of positive and negative integers, demonstrating their answers by manipulating the beans. Examples might include: $2 + 3 =$ _____, $7 + 1 =$ _____, $-8 - -3 =$ _____, $2 + -6 =$ _____. Students should be able to explain their solution to each problem to the class. Invite students to question, agree with, disagree with, or add to the ideas of their classmates.

Then give them something harder, such as $-3 - -7 =$ _____. Students are likely to say that they can't take away a negative 7 from a negative 3 because they don't have enough red beans. Circulate among the groups, listen to proposed solutions, and provide prompts as needed. Given enough time, some students are likely to realize that a white bean and a red bean together equal 0. They can add as many pairs of +1 and −1 as they need to without changing the value of 7 because they are just adding 0.

Realizing this, they will conclude that they have to add 4 red beans and 4 white beans in order to arrive at the correct answer of +4. When one group of students can demonstrate the correct answer using the beans, ask them to share the solution with the whole class. Provide other, similar problems so that all of the students can demonstrate the solution successfully.

Then use the EBG below to facilitate a discussion about the additive inverse property: that a number and its opposite equal zero. Although this activity is used in many classrooms across the country, most lesson plans (e.g., those available on the Internet) suggest that teachers feed the rule to the students rather than involve students in coming to articulate and understand the property underlying the rule. In contrast, the EBG below focuses on student thinking about the property rather than just the rule.

A discussion facilitated by this EBG requires students to think like mathematicians and use mathematical language and reasoning in order to develop an understanding of the additive inverse property. At the conclusion of the discussion, ask students to write their understanding of adding and subtracting positive and negative integers. The activity, as well as the discussion and writing that follow, will help students develop a rich understanding of the property while practicing using mathematical language and ways of reasoning.

## EBG for Bean Exercise to Demonstrate the Additive Inverse Property

*Stepping into a Text (the Bean Exercise)*

- What are you thinking?
- What questions do you have?
- How did it make you feel?

*Exploring the Text*

- What is a zero pair?
- When are zero pairs necessary?
- How would you explain this property to someone else?
- Why does a zero pair work?
- Does a zero pair always work?

*Stepping Back and Rethinking What You Know*

- Is there another way to demonstrate the solution?
- How does this idea fit with what you already know about adding and subtracting integers?
- Now that you understand how this works, where have you used this strategy before?

*Stepping Back and Objectifying the Experience*

- Is it better for you to memorize the rule or understand the property? Explain.
- Why does knowing the rule sometimes not help you solve the problem?
- Can you think of another way to demonstrate this property?

*Going Beyond*

- How does subtracting a negative integer apply to real life?

- Can you give a real-life example of using positive and negative integers?
- Can you give an example of this property outside of math class?

## AN ENVISIONMENT-BUILDING LESSON FOR ENGLISH LANGUAGE ARTS

Chapter 1 described a lesson that Johanna used to help develop student discussion skills. She paired a poem with an excerpt from a nonfiction text and used the T-chart in Table A.2 to support student thinking and writing about the texts. And the accompanying EBG helped her facilitate a discussion of that lesson.

| What do I understand from reading these two texts? What do I have questions about? What are my initial reactions to reading these texts? What are my first impressions? | After the discussion, what do I think about the two pieces now? How did my first impressions deepen or change? Who or what influenced my thinking? What questions do I have now? |
|---|---|
| | |

**Table A.2. T-Chart for Two Texts**

## EBG for "The Indian Child" and "from 'Unveiled'"

*Stepping into a Text*

- What are your first thoughts about the two pieces?
- What did you notice? What are these two pieces about? Do the pieces remind you of any other stories or poems you've read or heard?
- Is there a quote you can find that you think we might discuss?
- Do you have any questions that we might discuss?

*Exploring the Text*

- What do you think about the ending of each piece? How do the two pieces fit together?
- What is the lesson from the two pieces?
- What meaning do you attach to "from 'Unveiled'"?
- Think about the chapter from a white settler's perspective in the 1700s to mid-1800s. How might "The Indian Child" have affected the settler if it were available to read then?
- Would you like to be raised in either of these two cultures? Which one? Why? Why not?

*Stepping Back and Rethinking What You Know*

- Did anything from the two readings make you think of something that has happened to you in a different light? Explain.
- Does reading these two pieces increase your understanding of how cultures can be misunderstood? If so, how?
- What other issues in our society today do the writings make you think about in a different way? Explain.
- Did reading these two pieces make you think of childhood differently? What did you learn about childhood? How would you define childhood now after seeing it from these two different perspectives?

- How might a principal define childhood? A social worker? A parent? A child?
- What do you think of child raising now? Did the pieces make you think any differently about raising a child? Did you think of how you might like to raise your own children some day?

*Stepping Back and Objectifying the Experience*

- What effect did the style of the story and the style of the poem have on your understanding of the two pieces?
- What words were especially powerful for you? How did they add to your understanding of the two pieces?
- Does this story or the poem remind you of other pieces you've read? Which ones? How?
- Is the nonfiction chapter historically accurate? How do you know?
- What sources did the authors use?
- How are the poem and/or the chapter similar to other accounts you have read? How are they different?

*Going Beyond*

- How are the events of the chapter historically important?
- How are the ideas we have discussed in this classroom prevalent in the world today?
- What questions do "from 'Unveiled'" and "The Indian Child" raise for you now as a citizen of the United States?

# Appendix B

## Further Reading

Ackley, David, Laurie Farina, Monica Judd, Randall Roeser, and Eija Rougle. "Literacy across the Curriculum: A Team Approach to Promoting Critical Thinking." *Educator's Voice* 3 (Spring 2010): 2–9.

The authors describe their experience as an interdisciplinary team working to develop critical thinking in eighth graders. They worked with author Eija Rougle, a Partnership for Literacy coach, to incorporate into their instructional practice the key elements of minds-on instruction, substantive discussions, curricular connections, and critical thinking. Together they created a rubric, which they consistently used in each of their classrooms to promote and evaluate students' critical thinking. Their work is an example of the positive impact that teacher collaboration can have on students as they develop higher-order thinking skills.

Adler, Mary, and Eija Rougle. *Building Literacy through Classroom Discussion: Research-Based Strategies for Developing Critical Readers and Thoughtful Writers in Middle School.* New York: Scholastic, 2005.

Adler and Rougle summarize literacy research done by Judith Langer and Arthur Applebee and provide practical applications for the middle school classroom. The book focuses on ways that teachers can facilitate student conversation in order to promote higher-order thinking. This text was used extensively by the authors as they coached teachers on developing academic literacy and higher-order thinking in a variety of schools and school districts.

Applebee, Arthur N. *Curriculum as Conversation: Transforming Traditions of Teaching and Learning.* Chicago: University of Chicago Press, 1996.

Applebee presents a view of curriculum that stresses knowledge in action versus knowledge out of context. Drawing on a series of studies, he argues that the knowledge that matters to students is gained by serving as apprentices in the discipline at hand. Rather than doing social studies, the student learns the ways of thinking and doing of a social scientist. Applebee posits that by engaging in important curricular conversations that are high quality, contain enough material to sustain extended discussion, and focus on interrelated ideas, students will not only learn the content of a discipline but also the ways of thinking and doing that bring the content to life. Applebee's research and thinking provide the foundation. He describes real examples from classrooms across the country.

Common Core State Standards Initiative. *Preparing America's Students for College and Career.* 2015. http://www.corestandards.org.

The national Common Core website describes the Common Core State Standards for English language arts (ELA) and mathematics, as well as the literacy standards for history/social studies, science, and technical subjects. The website provides extensive information for school leaders, teachers, and parents.

Langer, Judith A. *Envisioning Knowledge: Building Literacy in the Academic Disciplines.* New York: Teachers College Press, 2011.

In this text, Langer extends her earlier work and examines how students gain knowledge and become literate within the academic areas. She defines *disciplinary literacy* and provides a framework to guide students to develop a deep understanding of content, as well as the ways of thinking, speaking, and writing appropriate to each discipline. The text focuses on the need for knowledge development rather than information collection, which is essential for today's students. Langer provides many classroom examples that demonstrate this approach.

Langer, Judith A. *Envisioning Literature: Literary Understanding and Literature Instruction.* New York: Teachers College Press, 1995; 2nd ed., 2011.

In this book, Langer introduces envisionment building—the way the mind works to build an understanding of a literary work. Based on years of research, including that of the National Research Center on Literature Teaching and Learning, she describes the options or stances a person takes as he or she develops an interpretation of a text. An envisionment-building classroom scaffolds ways for all of the students to participate in the discussion because the thinking of each student extends and deepens the thinking of the others. In light of this research, Langer proposes new ways to think about instruction as teachers incorporate the multiple perspectives that emerge from class discussion.

Langer, Judith A., with Elizabeth Close, Janet Angelis, and Paula Preller. *Guidelines for Teaching Middle and High School Students to Read and Write Well: Six Features of Effective Instruction.* Albany, NY: Center on English Learning & Achievement, September 2000. http://www.albany.edu/cela/publication/guidebook.htm.

The guidelines presented in this freely available booklet are based on Langer's research in which she compared typical English programs with those that achieved outstanding results. She identified six features of instruction that are effective in developing student achievement in reading, writing, and other important literacy skills in classrooms across the country. Classroom examples as well as an analysis of activities that work illustrate each feature.

Langer, Judith A., and Elizabeth Close. *Improving Literary Understanding through Classroom Conversation*. Albany, NY: National Research Center on English Learning and Achievement, 2001. http://www.albany.edu/cela/publication/env/pdf.

This booklet, available for downloading, summarizes the findings of the National Research Center on Literature Teaching and Learning. It explains the difference in reading for literary understanding and reading for information, as well as ways to enrich literary understanding. It describes classroom strategies that support students before, during, and after they participate in a literary discussion.

# Literary Works Cited

*Among the Brave*. Margaret Peterson Haddix. New York: Simon and Schuster, 2004.
*An Angel for Solomon Singer*. Cynthia Rylant. New York: Orchard Books, 1992.
*Because of Winn-Dixie*. Kate DiCamillo. Cambridge, MA: Candlewick Press, 2000.
"The Cell." Bill Bryson. In *A Short History of Nearly Everything*. New York: Random House, 2003.
"Charles." Shirley Jackson. In *The Lottery and Other Stories*. New York: Farrar, Straus, and Giroux, 2005.
*Encounter*. Jane Yolen. New York: Harcourt Brace Jovanovich, 1992.
"from 'Unveiled.'" Gladys Alam Saroyan. In *The Flag of Childhood: Poems from the Middle East*, edited by Naomi Shihab Nye. New York: Aladdin Paperback, 2002.
*The Gift of the Magi*. O. Henry. New York: Hawthorn Books, 1972.
*The Giver*. Lois Lowry. Boston: Houghton Mifflin, 1993.
*If the World Were a Village: A Book about the World's People*. David J. Smith and Shelagh Armstrong. Toronto: Kids Can Press, 2011.
"The Indian Child." C. Neidhammer. In *Daughters of the Earth: The Lives and Legends of Native American Indian Women*. New York: Touchstone/Simon and Schuster, 1977.
"A Lesson for Kings." Anonymous. A fable from India.
*Lies and Other Tall Tales*. Christopher Myers. Collected by Zora Neale Hurston. New York: HarperCollins, 2005.
*Midnight Magic*. Avi. New York: Scholastic Press, 1999.
*The Red Book*. Barbara Lehman. Boston: Houghton Mifflin, 2004.
*Stand Tall, Molly-Lou Melon*. Patty Lovell. New York: Putnam, 2001.
*Stellaluna*. Janell Cannon. San Diego: Harcourt Brace Jovanovich, 1993.

*The Toll-Bridge Troll.* Patricia Rae Wolff and Kimberly Bulcken Root. New York: Voyage Books, 2000.

# Bibliography

Abrami, Philip C., Robert M. Bernard, Eugene Borokhovski, David I. Waddington, C. Anne Wade, and Tonje Persson. "Strategies for Teaching Students to Think Critically: A Meta-Analysis." *Review of Educational Research* 85, no. 2 (2015): 275–314.

Ackley, David, Laurie Farina, Monica Judd, Randall Roeser, and Eija Rougle. "Literacy across the Curriculum: A Team Approach to Promoting Critical Thinking." *Educator's Voice* 3 (Spring 2010): 2–9.

Adler, Mary, and Eija Rougle. *Building Literacy through Classroom Discussion: Research-Based Strategies for Developing Critical Readers and Thoughtful Writers in Middle School*. New York: Scholastic, 2005.

Angelis, Janet I., Johanna Shogan, Laura Carroll, April Ordway, Nicole Hunt, and Angela Spanakos. "Engaging Special Education Students in Higher Levels of Literacy." *Educator's Voice* 2 (2009): 2–13.

Angelis, Janet I., and Kristen C. Wilcox. "Poverty, Performance, and Frog Ponds: What Best Practice Research Tells Us about Their Connections." *Kappan* 13, no. 3 (2011): 26–31.

Applebee, Arthur N. *Curriculum as Conversation: Transforming Traditions of Teaching and Learning*. Chicago: University of Chicago Press, 1996.

Applebee, Arthur N., and Judith A. Langer. "A Snapshot of Writing Instruction in Middle Schools and High Schools." *English Journal* 100, no. 6 (2011): 14–27.

———. *Writing Instruction That Works: Proven Methods for Middle and High School Classrooms*. New York: Teachers College Press, 2014.

Applebee, Arthur N., Judith A. Langer, Martin Nystrand, and Adam Gamoran. "Discussion-Based Approaches to Developing Understanding: Classroom Instruction and Student Performance in Middle and High School English." *American Educational Research Journal* 40, no. 3 (Fall 2003): 685–730.

Bakhtin, Mikhail. *The Dialogic Imagination: Four Essays*. Austin: University of Texas Press, 1992.

Bereiter, Carl, and Marlene Scardamalia. *The Psychology of Written Composition*. Hillsdale, NJ: Erlbaum, 1987.

Biancarosa, Gina, and Catherine E. Snow. *Reading Next—a Vision for Action and Research in Middle and High School Literacy: A Report to the Carnegie Corporation of New York*. Washington, DC: Alliance for Excellent Education, 2004.

Bolter, Jay D. *Writing Space: The Computer, Hypertext, and the History of Writing*. Hillsdale, NJ: Lawrence Erlbaum Associates, 1991.

Bryk, Anthony, and Barbara Schneider. *Trust in Schools: A Core Resource for Improvement*. New York: Russell Sage Foundation, 2002.

Close, Elizabeth, Molly Hull, and Judith A. Langer. "Writing and Reading Relationships in Literacy Learning: Theory and Research in Practice." In *Learning to Write, Writing to Learn*, edited by Roselmina Indrisano and Jeanne R. Paratore. Newark, DE: International Reading Association, 2005.

Common Core State Standards Initiative. *Common Core State Standards for English Language Arts and Literacy in History/Social Studies, Science, and Technical Subjects*. Washington, DC: National Governors Association and Council of Chief State School Officers, 2010.

Danielson, Charlotte. *Enhancing Student Achievement: A Framework for School Improvement*. Alexandria, VA: Association for Supervision and Curriculum Development, 2002.

Dweck, Carol. *Mindset: The New Psychology of Success*. New York: Random House, 2006.

Engel, Susan. "Playing to Learn." *New York Times*, February 2, 2010. http://www.nytimes.com/2010/02/02/opinion/02engel.html.

English, Fenwick. *Deciding What to Teach and Test: Developing, Aligning, and Leading the Curriculum*. 3rd ed. Thousand Oaks, CA: Corwin, 2010.

Grossman, Pamela L., Peter Smagorinsky, and Sheila Valencia. "Appropriating Tools for Teaching English: A Theoretical Framework for Research on Learning to Teach." *American Journal of Education* 108, no. 1 (1999): 1–29.

Hakim, Joy. *A History of Us: The First Americans*. New York: Oxford University Press, 2009.

Johnston, Peter. *Opening Minds: Using Language to Change Lives*. Portland, ME: Stenhouse, 2012.

King, Dan. "Drummer Boys: Creating Historical Fiction and Studying Historical Documents." *Middle Level Learning*, May/June 2010: 10–12.

Langer, Judith A. *Envisioning Knowledge: Building Literacy in the Academic Disciplines*. New York: Teachers College Press, 2011.

———. *Envisioning Literature: Literary Understanding and Literature Instruction*. New York: Teachers College Press, 1995. 2nd ed., 2011.

———. *Getting to Excellent: How to Create Better Schools*. New York: Teachers College Press, 2004.

Langer, Judith A., Elizabeth Close, Janet Angelis, and Paula Preller. *Guidelines for Teaching Middle and High School Students to Read and Write Well*. Albany, NY: Center on English Learning and Achievement, 2000. http://www.albany.edu/cela/publication/brochure/guidelines.pdf.

Murphy, MaryAnn. "Envisionment Building in Math: A Reflection on the Year." *The Partnership Community* 3, no. 1 (2010): 3. www.albany.edu/cela/publication/p4l_newletter_10_2010.pdf.

Muth, Jon J. *The Three Questions*. New York: Scholastic, 2002.

Newkirk, Thomas. "Teachers: Know When to Stop Talking." *Education Week*, July 28, 2015. http://www.edweek.org/ew/articles/2015/07/28/teachers-know-when-to-stop-talking.html?qs=july+28,+2015+inmeta:gsaentity_Source%2520URL%2520entities%3DEducation%2520Week%2520Articles+inmeta:genre%3DOpinion+inmeta:Authors%3DThomas%2520Newkirk.

99U. "Simon Sinek: Why Leaders Eat Last." YouTube presentation, December 4, 2013. https://www.youtube.com/watch?v=ReRcHdeUG9Y.

Nystrand, Martin. *Opening Dialogue: Understanding the Dynamics of Language and Learning in the English Classroom*. New York: Teachers College Press, 1996.

Nystrand, Martin, Lawrence Wu, Adam Gamoran, Susie Zeiser, and Daniel Long. "Questions in Time: Investigating the Structure and Dynamics of Unfolding Classroom Discourse." *Discourse Processes* 35 (March–April 2003): 135–96.

Partnership for 21st Century Skills. *Partnership for 21st Century Skills, Education and Competitiveness: A Resource and Policy Guide*. Tucson, AZ: Partnership for 21st Century Skills, 2004.

Rogoff, Barbara. *Apprenticeship in Thinking: Cognitive Development in Social Context*. New York: Oxford University Press, 1990.

Scardamalia, Marlene. "Transforming Teaching and Learning through Technology: Which Way to the Revolution?" Presentation, University at Albany, State University of New York, Albany, November 1, 2012.

Shanahan, Cynthia, and Timothy Shanahan. "Does Disciplinary Literacy Have a Place in Elementary School?" *Reading Teacher* 67, no. 8 (2014): 636–39. doi:10.1002/trtr.1257.

Shanahan, Timothy, and Cynthia Shanahan. "Teaching Disciplinary Literacy to Adolescents: Rethinking Content-Area Literacy." *Harvard Educational Review* 78, no. 1 (Spring 2008): 40–59.

Szymborska, Wislawa. "The Poet and the World." Lecture, Nobel Prize in Literature Ceremony, Stockholm, Sweden, December 7, 1996.

Wilcox, Kristen C. *What Works in Middle School Science: Preparing Students to Become the Next Generation of Scientists*. Albany: State University of New York, 2009. http://www.albany.edu/nykids/files/MiddleSchool_Science_FullReport.pdf.

Wilcox, Kristen C., and Janet I. Angelis. *Best Practices from High-Performing Middle Schools: How Successful Schools Remove Obstacles and Create Pathways to Learning*. New York: Teachers College Press, 2009.

Wilcox, Kristen C., Hal A. Lawson, and Janet I. Angelis. "Classroom, School, and District Impacts on Diverse Student Literacy Achievement." *Teachers College Record* 117, no. 9 (2015): 1–38.

Wilcox, Kristen C., Hal A. Lawson, Karen Gregory, Janet I. Angelis, Francesca T. Durand, Kathryn S. Schiller, Sarah Zuckerman, and Nisa Felicia. *Comparing and Contrasting Odds-Beating Schools: Toward a Theory of Action*. Albany: State University of New York, 2015. http://www.albany.edu/nykids/files/brief.TOA.NYKids.pdf.

www.ingramcontent.com/pod-product-compliance
Lightning Source LLC
Chambersburg PA
CBHW031552300426
44111CB00006BA/278